MOTHER GOOSE MEETS A WOMAN CALLED WISDOM

Mother Goose

Meets a Woman Called Wisdom

A Short Course in
the Art of Self-Determination

ᚼᚼ

LINDA H. HOLLIES

UNITED CHURCH PRESS
Cleveland, Ohio

United Church Press, Cleveland, Ohio 44115
© 2000 by Linda H. Hollies

All rights reserved. Published 2000

Printed in the United States of America on acid-free paper

05   04   03   02   01   00   5   4   3   2   1

Library of Congress Cataloging-in-Publication Data

Hollies, Linda H.
    Mother Goose meets a woman called wisdom: a short course in the art of
self-determination / by Linda H. Hollies.
        p.   cm.
    ISBN 0-8298-1348-9 (cloth : alk. paper)
    1. Christian women—Religious life.   2. Autonomy (Psychology)—
Religious aspects—Christianity.   3. Nursery rhymes.   I. Title.
BV4527.H653   1999
2422.643—dc21   99-41005
                                                                            CIP

Dedicated to my personal sages and women of wisdom!

Mama, Doretha Robinson Adams; Big Mama, Eunice Robinson Wade; Granny, Lucinda Robinson Weston, my life sources

Barbara Jean Baker Vinson, Darlene Sims Lee, and Elizabeth Clark Brown, my school years' best friends

Ms. Ethel Sims, Ms. Catherine Jones, and Aunt Sweetie, neighborhood "mothers"

Thelma Nunn Pryor and Madine Blakley, lifelong church sistas

Hortense House and Della Burt, teachers/mentors, friends

Emma Justes and Emilie Townes, seminary profs, role models

JoClare Wilson and Cynthia Smitko, clinical pastoral education guides and pushers

Helen Marie Fannings Ammons and Marilyn Magee, "sista-mothers"-friends

Linda Foster Mumson, Barbara Issacs, and Cecelia Long, North Illinois path clearers

Fran Brandon, Ida Easley, Michelle Cobb, and Brenda Heffner, Garrett-Evangelical Theological Seminary prayer group

Marie Antoinette Carson, great woman, good friend

Vera Jo Edington and Joyce E. Wallace, Twinkling Butterfly Club

Harlene Harden, who loves me unconditionally

Valerie Bridgeman Davis and Genevieve Brown, who were personal prophets in calling me to fly!

Daisybelle Thomas Quinney and Janet Hopkins, sisthurs

Eleanor L. Miller, my pastor and intercessor

Lucille Brown, Ruby Earven, and Ray Margaret Jackson, surrogate mothers, sages, and women of wisdom

Contents

⊱⊰⊱

Preface

⊱⊰⊱⊰

W ITH GREAT FANFARE and creativity the producer had the set built to specifications of striking proportions. Nothing like it had ever been seen before. Those who were to play minor and supporting roles were brought on board. The script called for two main characters, whose parts would greatly influence the overall production. They had to be the most perfect specimens of their time. The high excitement, thrilling drama, and magnificent set would overshadow them if they were not superbly matched to carry off their roles. The two were hand picked and dominated the center stage with enough energy that the others could simply respond to their lead.

After a stunning publicity campaign had been orchestrated, the names of the two leading characters were released. Adam and Eve, let your story begin! With them, the story of God's interactions with the world unfurled. The drama began in the Garden of Eden and has been continually unfolding, changing plots and twists every day since. The characters change, but the story remains basically the same.

The name of the first book of the Christian canon of Scripture, Genesis, means "the beginning." And it starts with the familiar words, "In the beginning God created . . ." The activities of the Creator are detailed for our knowledge, our education, and our appreciation of this world in which we live. Moses, another character whose life has touched ours, compiled and wrote the story of our ancient past. Being male, he told it from his worldview. We have a powerful male producer, God. There is a powerful male villain, the serpent. A tall, dark, handsome, gullible, and silent male figure, Adam, is present. But the one whose story has never been told is Mother Eve. Others have told her story, but always from their vantage point in history. Adam was the first one who pointed the finger of blame at Eve, and her story has been a twisted plot and evil tale since. Yet we know that Eve lived and impacted the world. Eve has her own story!

A story relates our personal and individual history. A story ties us to the universal plot of life and other characters. A story is an invitation for us to connect with others whose lives are similar and yet unlike our own. A story reveals the dramatic, the tragic, the wonderful, the comedic, the horrific, and what is awesome in our existence. All stories do not have "happily ever after" endings. Such endings occur only in slapstick comedies. The girls and women we meet in Mother Goose and in Holy Scripture are most often victims, in tragic circumstances, with seemingly no resources. These sisters have stories that reveal challenges, questions, pain, mystery, and searching, and their stories provide strong evidence of their self-determination. As we read their stories and ponder their lives we can gain both new knowledge and strategies from their collective wisdom. Their stories allow us to become more authentic and better able to replicate their self-determination in our daily lives.

All stories need both a teller and a listener. There has to be someone who will share the events and someone who will be an active listener, receiving the details without judgment, censorship, or criticism. Stories are gifts to be shared. Storytelling is the gift of self-disclosure. When others can hear our stories with openness and comprehension, we can take off our masks and come out of hiding. Women have been forced to lie, to build defenses, and to "act" within certain prescribed manners because no one wanted to listen to their "real and honest" stories. "Everybody" already knew the collected oral myths about Eve. Whenever they were told, her "sin" grew larger, and her fable became more notorious. By the time the canon was compiled, there was little debate about her role in this familiar story. Eve has never had the opportunity to tell her story and share her wisdom.

Eve's story is older than our recorded history. It is older than the myths, fables, and fairy tales we have in hand-me-down collections. For the story of God is older than the one recorded by Moses. Our story line is part of the ancient story that directly connects us to the Life Source. Our story is tied to Mother Eve whom God created with sensitivity, care, love, power, intelligence, and dominion. The planning of a grand design for Eve's life, and ours, predates that of the creation stories attributed to Moses that we have in Scripture.

Stories are not limited to the powerful survivors of the world's history. The weak, the insignificant, and the victimized have their stories too. Stories fulfill our basic curiosity about our past and our beginnings. Stories help us to utilize our imagination to "see" from where we have emerged. Stories entertain. Stories keep our customs, values, beliefs, hopes, and dreams alive. Women of every nation, race, tribe, and ethnic group have stories to tell. Their stories have been passed down through the oral tradition. They have been retold as fables of exploit and collected as the myths of our sheroes. Eve and too many other foremothers have been erased and made silent for too long. In these pages, they speak in a different voice. In these pages, they teach us a short course through their own feats of self-determination. They had a teacher, instructor, and guide who was also "in the beginning." Their experiences are truths revealed by Lady Wisdom in their time and for our times.

How would the women of myths, fables, and fairy tales reveal themselves to us? If you have an open mind, a seeking spirit, and space for the new and different, these girlfriends will offer you a new glimpse of their lives. Ask them questions. Press them for insight. Encourage them to help you return to your "beginning," and let a new story begin!

AUTHOR'S NOTE ABOUT SCRIPTURES

I take great personal liberty with Scripture! I believe it was written for me. And I know it needs to have inclusive language to include all of us. So I have attempted to be true to documenting the sources of every scriptural reference, using the New International Version translation for most of my references. However, this version is not wholly inclusive in its language. Therefore, I pray you will be indulgent as you read your select version and find it does not say "exactly" what I have stated. It's what I saw and felt was intended!

ACKNOWLEDGMENTS

"How rich and glorious is the portion God offers us. . . . How vast are the resources of God's power open to us who have faith" (Eph. 1:18–19).

This is to acknowledge the vast and wonderful network of folk who have touched my life and shared their love, care, prayers, and wise counsel with me. A page cannot contain their names. A book could not hold their gifts. Only eternity will be able to reveal my "rich and glorious portion of kin, friend and family"! Yet, list some names I must.

My parents, James and Doretha Adams; grandparents, Big Mama, Eunice Wade, and Dock Wade. Nanny Mama, Lucinda Weston, surrogate parents and friends, Clinton and Barbara Weston. To the most loving sisters in the whole wide world, Jackie Brodie Davis (Bob and Troy), Riene Adams Morris (Tony/Lynn; Mike/Missy), Regina Pleasant (Ray, Raymond, Ibn.). To my most handsome brothers, James Jr. (Jeannette, Noah, and Mohanna), Eddie (Onnette, Eddie Jr., Candance), David Joel (Kim, David Jr., Ean), and Robert (Lisa, Maxwell). To my father in ministry, Rev. James Anderson; my "tutors," Rev. Bill Cull and Rev. David Nelson; my bishop-brother-friend, Jonathan D. Keaton and his wife, Bev. To "Da Boys" who hold my back, brothers, friends, and colleagues, Dr. Zawdie K. Abiade (Nancy), Rev. Anthony Earl (Bobbie), Dr. Michael Carson (Katherine), Dr. Dennis Robinson (Darlene), and Dr. Donald Guest (Brenda). To my primary cheerleaders, Kim Sadler, Linda Peavy, Carol

Greet, and Deborah Robertson. To my "newest sista" artist, Synthia Saint James. To the very best administrative assistant in the whole wide world, Eric Thorsen! And to my "living large" ebonics instructor, Wezzie Martin!

I also give God thanks for Veronese Strader and Nora Meredith, Trudy Henry, Millard Mallard, Corene Speller, Ora Robertson, Ms. Heard, Ms. Magnolia, Phyllis Jackson, and all the sisters of the Albion District, especially; and for the West Michigan Conference United Methodist Women, in particular, President Julia Deemer, and Dean Chris Bobier, who have helped me birth this project into existence and kept loving me during an insane period in my life! During this same time, Rev. Marge Berman waltzed into my life with Azariah!

My family is another name for God's Tangible Love! Mista Chuck is my soul mate and my very best friend. His children have included me in their family circle. Wisdom demands that I name them: Pam and Erin, JoAnne, Paul, Lacie, Cory, and Darian "Bear"; Donna, Ronald Charles, and Anita.

Finally, Wisdom has called me through my children of the womb: Gregory Raymond Everett; Grelon Renard Everett; my hook-'em-up beautician daughter, Grian Eunyke and her children, Giraud Chase, Gamel Chasad, and Ms. Music, Symphony; and the children of my heart, Jacquie Ford, Tracy Flaggs, Darlene Webster, and Sandy Adams. I pray Wisdom enfolds them tightly!

Introduction

⊱⊰⊱⊰

Dear Dr. Hollies:

I have procrastinated a long time before writing you this letter. I always wanted to, but each time fear overcame me and the words seemed to escape me. Now, I wish I had confronted the fear and just did it, but hindsight has that way of giving you 20/20 vision.

Anyway, about three (3) weeks ago a detective came to the church where I was working looking for me because the church I used to work at had signed warrants for my arrest. I was there when he came, but the church secretary told him I was not.

Immediately, I called my pastor and asked him to meet me at the church. When he came, he called around to find out what was going on. He discovered, what I already knew, that money was missing from the church. A number of other calls began to come to him following that one. Once the telephone stopped ringing and the office emptied out . . . then I did too. I had to tell the truth about being guilty of the crimes of which I was being accused.

In some ways, I was extremely frightened and in other ways I was relieved. I spent the next week crying and praying. (Sometimes I find myself still crying and praying.) So, currently I am out, on bond, awaiting whatever lies ahead for me legally. I am not too concerned about the legalities because God has already shown mighty power in this episode. God called me and I answered. For years, God has been calling me and offering me a way out, but I did not know God then. I was too ignorant to run toward God, so I ran away. Now, I'm tired of running.

I have an opportunity to be free like I have never experienced before. For the past four months God has been showing me myself. I'm discovering the real me, the person that I truly am and not the person that I created for myself. In this, God is giving me an opportunity to step out of the prison I placed myself in some sixteen years ago and to be and become all of what I have only dreamed and verbally declared.

I know that I have lost a great many friends and even greater is the trust many people will lose in me. I can deal with that because I know that from this I can be true to myself, I can stop feeling lonely because I can let people know who I am, and I can get the help I have needed so desperately for so very long.

You and my pastor are the only persons I have ever told, but I never attended graduate school, had no job offer from that major industry, never attended Catholic school, and I barely know my parents, so I never knew my grandparents. My "creative life" grew bigger and bigger with every lie. I never thought about truth telling and living until I came to really know Christ. There were many times when I tried to be myself, but then someone else came along and told the lie I'd told them. As I grew and came to know and understand Christ—I wanted to live. I didn't want to be scared anymore. I didn't want to run, to hide, to lie anymore and now I don't have to.

I am very sorry to have to tell you this. I wanted to be "special" and more than the "ordinary person" I am. But today I realize that convincing other people what I was did not make me those things. I am delighted that this is happening now, because . . . it's not too late. I have another chance, and I'm going to take it.

One day at a time is what I am dealing with right now. In so many ways, I am coming to realize that God has been fighting for me a long time and I never knew. Ironically, this happened after the women's retreat, but I really needed to be there. So many of the events that transpired that weekend have really strengthened me and have allowed me to see beyond the pain I am having to endure.

I thank you for allowing me to be a part of a caring network of sisters. After the conference I have maintained relationships with some of the ladies there and my "network of Angels" has ministered to me in my weakest hours. And they never knew. Just being yourselves has made me be so much more than I was.

Sometimes, I feel saddened in this ordeal, because I think I should feel broken, or depressed. But I don't. More accurately, I feel like the bowed lady in Luke, and now I am standing straight. I may be premature in claiming the victory, but I know that it's mine.

Only God knows what lies ahead for me; so in the event I don't see you at the next gathering, please keep me in your prayers. Know that something kept me away, but if it is God's will, I will be there. I surely want to be.

Although I might have done some bad things, please don't ever believe that I did them for bad reasons. I love people, and I love helping people and working with people. That is what I do. (Perhaps, that is the spiritual gift I possess.) I always put others first, believing that I always had time to take care of myself. Now I realize that until I deal with my own "stuff," I cannot be nearly as effective in helping someone else.

Once again, I thank you for all of your love and guidance. You are an angel.

Please keep me in your prayers.

Yours in Christ,

Your Lil' Sister

Dear Lil' Sister,

Thanks for trusting me with your story. I confess that you had me fooled. You convinced me, an "old pro," that you had it going on. You told your story with conviction, with passion, and with gusto. You are an awesome young woman. And your honesty makes you more tremendous in my view. For, if the truth is told, I've been there and done that too! I have lived a lie, based on some myth, for so long that I believed it and, like you, had others believing it too! So, Lil' Sister, don't be discouraged. I know firsthand of your story! It's not new. It's not surprising. And it's not unique. Most of us live lives of lies! Too many of us, your big sisters, have been where you are, and to be honest, we haven't moved that far away! So, I find it refreshing, life-giving, and hopeful that at your young age you have already discovered that a life built upon fantasy and fairy tales does not have a "happily ever after" ending! Welcome to the real world. It's good to have you with us.

I dedicate this volume of truth to you. I dedicate this volume of honest, hard facts to the millions of us who have discovered and are continuing to uncover reality based upon our faith in God. I dedicate this volume of old stories, based upon old wisdom, to those of us who have lived old lives based upon old fading dreams, ancient broken promises, and tattered, unrealistic expectations. The God who created us, loves us, and has grand hopes for us comes again, offering us new views of our lives, new options for our today, and new hope for our tomorrows. Lil' Sister, God's got your back! Thanks for sharing with me. Together, we will share with others! Perhaps others will join our "new women's society" of myth debunkers and fairy-tale destroyers! There's much work to be done. There are millions of sisters to be saved. So, Girlfriend, we had best get busy!

Know that I continue to pray your strength in God. Be bold. Be bodacious. Be yourself!

Shalom,
Sista Linda

Why a Book on
Self-Determination?

ᚻᚻᚻᚻ

AFTER THE CONFERENCE IS over, when you can't remember the theme or the keynote speaker's name; when once again, you reach that place in your spiritual existence where the hope of glory seems dim and far away; when the assurance of your salvation is fading fast and when the absurdity, called life, is threatening to cloud your skies and overflow your eyes; when you can't hear anybody pray and can't seem to get a prayer through, what do you do?

When the heavens have turned to glass and you recognize that it is a pitch-black night in your own soul; when you sing the songs, say the words of the creeds, recite the prayer as if it's an old, familiar nursery rhyme, and the interior emptiness remains and you feel as if your spiritual well has gone dry, what then?

When the fantasy you have lived out and followed begins to fall apart; when the fairy tale's conquering hero doesn't appear; when the picket fence has wood that's dry-rotted and the cute little cottage is leaning on its foundation, how do you pick up all the broken and scattered pieces of your dreams and move on?

Sisters, this is called standing at the crossroads of life, wondering which way to go. When you reach points such as these, you know it's time for change. It's time to rewrite the story. It's time to reframe the picture. It's time to reorient yourself to a new reality. It's time to diss the myths. It's time to debunk the fairy tales. It's time to come out of the castle of make-believe and begin to walk by faith toward a new future. The first thing we have to do is acknowledge the truth that our particular fairy tale has come to a less than grand conclusion. And we sit down, have a good cry, and describe for ourselves what we have learned from the harsh lessons of our lives, for every circumstance comes to teach us. If we don't master the lesson, we will repeat the same scene! Fairy tales do have lives of their own. They will continually try to reconstruct themselves for a repeat performance! They don't mind us doing a series of reruns.

When we face the reality of our lives, we begin the difficult task of making some new choices. We achieve this movement in our lives by coming to some different sets of conclusions. We decide to take some risks, to learn some new strategies, and to listen for the voice of Wisdom to guide our steps.

Each of us is on a journey. The paths are different. The routes are diverse. The courses will vary. For each of us is a pilgrim, seeking inner peace, wholeness, and unconditional love. We all arrive at the crossroads of life. It is at the crossroads, the juncture where yesterday meets tomorrow, the point where "used to" meets "never again," that we make serious decisions in our lives. This is a book for you when you reach the crossroads.

Standing at the juncture of "should I?" and "I don't dare," wondering which direction to take, causes great emotional pain. Although we so easily say, "Been there, done that," at a crossroads, we usually choose to return to the familiar. "Been there, done that" should have taught us that the familiar did not satisfy in the past. But there is something predictable about a crisis; it will pull us back into whatever has brought comfort in the past. That's why we so often find ourselves doing the same things again and again. We even ask ourselves, "Didn't I just come through this scene?" Yet we seem to think that if we do it one more time, we can get different results. Huh?

We continue to go back to the familiar because going in a different direction requires entering into the very heart of the crisis—what our mothers used to call the eye of the storm. And doing this requires taking a serious, honest, and open look at the pain, hurt, and misery living within. Most of us have a difficult time even saying, "I hurt." It's more acceptable to say, "I'm angry or mad," because it "feels" as if we are more in control! It's a lie, for hurt and anger are two sides of the same coin.

We have become experts at stuffing, compacting, and hiding from the junk that has accumulated in our emotional reservoirs. Reservoirs are holding places. They don't have the means to allow in what is fresh and new. Reservoirs have no outlets, so they become places that collect our aging, stagnant, stinking junk until it has offensive odors. In times of crisis we will do the external things that keep us stuck at the crossroads. We will hide, deny, lie, cover up, and backtrack into the familiar. But the familiar will only bring us right back to the crossroads. Here, Amazing Grace continues to woo us to change directions. At the crossroads, the Lifegiver pleads with us to risk going in another way. The God of additional chances is determined that we risk, by faith, the opportunities to try new avenues, for we have returned to the same crossroads.

David, the psalmist, says so distinctly, "Yea, though I walk through the valley of the shadow of death, I will fear no evil" (Ps. 23). But most of us try with all our might to walk around, bypass, and avoid the valley. We fear being exposed to the world without having all the right answers. We fear being vulnerable and appearing weak before our peers. We fear leaving our comfort zones, for we don't know what's on "the other side." Fear keeps us hidden. Fear robs us of our spiritual, emotional, and physical vitality. And fear keeps us returning to the same crossroads.

This is a book about standing at the crossroads. This is a book about facing, confronting, and destroying the fairy tales and the fantasies that have controlled our thinking, our actions, and our life-denying behaviors. This is a book about new possibilities. This is a book about the sweet mystery of life. This is a book about risk taking, leaping with faith, and laughing as you discover new truth for your own life. This is a book about challenging the status quo and "the way it's always been" said or done. This is a book about "what would have happened if . . ."

and "what will happen when . . ." This is a book about coping with crisis. This is a book about resolving many of the conflicts that have kept us from moving forward. This is a book about self-determination, self-definition, and self-discovery.

My call to ministry is the pastoral care of souls. My specialty in ministry is the inner healing of women. I delight in leading folks toward inner healing, the discipline that calls us to look within and to face the past, learn from it, and grow into better tomorrows. Inner healing is a ministry reminding us that God is great enough, kind enough, majestic enough, and willing enough to walk with us through the mess of our past and allow the correcting work we need to occur. Inner healing is the work of the Holy Spirit, which is both mystical and mysterious. Inner healing is both unexplainable and yet able to be articulated. Inner healing is a journey through the crossroads. It is a retelling of the old story. It is a new look at old stuff. It is learning from the past in order to journey with spiritual vitality, emotional energy, and wholeness.

God loves us just the way we are, filled with the fantasies, fairy tales, and myths that keep us stuck at the crossroads of life. And God loves us too much to leave us the way we are.

So, another book; a fresh view of many of the fairy tales, myths, fables, and fantasies we have grown up hearing and have internalized so well. So, another book; a different look at the wisdom of the Holy Scriptures and an unconventional view of the lives of many familiar characters.

I invite you to explore the mystery of life with me. I bid you to examine new options, new strategies, and new methods for making decisions at your crossroads. I solicit you to be open to the pregnant possibilities that can be experienced in your life. Come and see. Come and be stretched. Come and be challenged. Come and learn. Come and grow. Come and be changed. A woman named Wisdom invites you to come!

LET US PRAY

Omnipotent Ancient of Days, Miraculous Miracle Worker, and Sweet Potentate of Power, we join our hearts to worship you. Creator of our essence, Redeemer of our lives, and Great Lover of our souls, we pause now to honor you. Matchless Friend of sinners, Ultimate Hope of the penitent, and Awesome Deliverer, we long to bless your name.

Balm in Gilead, Comforter of hurting hearts, and Mender of wounded spirits, we dare to enter your throne room with boldness. You have invited us to come and we linger in your presence. From the rising of the sun to the going down of its rays, you alone are worthy of our praise. All day long you make sweet love to us. You whisper tender words in the wind. You bathe us in your love and perfume us with rich wisdom. You light our fires with more intimate knowledge of ourselves. Only you stroke our faltering self-esteem and kiss us deeply with your Living Word. Although our fairy tales have fallen down around our ankles and we can feel pretty low at times, you have been a consistent Lover. You remain tender, gentle, and thorough as you prop us up, build us up, and touch us in the right place, at the right time, assuring us that "everything will be all right."

Now, we just stop and return the favor of your love. We want to pause and linger with passionate "thank you's" falling from our lips. Receive the love from the depths of our souls, even as we stand at another crossroads, wondering again which direction we should take. Lead us. Guide us in paths that lead us to new life! In the name of Jesus the Christ we pray and believe. May it be so now and always!

PERSPECTIVE

The journey to this particular work began with a group of women, sisters, who asked me to be their "epiphany storyteller." It was the gathering of wise women. This theme came from our collective insight around the Betty LaDuke artwork used as the cover of my book *Jesus and Those Bodacious Women*. Sister Betty has created a strong visual image: a group of determined women, dark and faceless, with walking sticks in hand, shepherding animals and bringing with them a small child. Above the women flies a dove, the Christian symbol for the Holy Spirit. The reflection of the dove shines, like a cross, in the forehead of every woman in the picture. Betty's creation birthed in me the questions: What would've happened if the wise men had been wise women? What sort of gifts would women have brought Mary? What wisdom would they have imparted to the mother of the Savior? What kinds of stories would each one have shared about the journey to womanhood and motherhood? Would one of them have been a single woman? A widow? Who was this child with them? What made them take this long and difficult journey of many years?

These questions haunted me. The images stirred me. My periods of prayerful reflection, careful research, and delightful chatting with diverse groups of women became a time for spinning another universal yarn of biblical women's experiences that are not recorded in the tapestry of the canon. Whether African American, Hispanic, or Anglo, each group stated, "You know they would have said . . . you know they would have brought . . . you know they would have done . . ." The stories of women are inexplicably interwoven, although they are told in the different voices that reflect our individual cultures and worldviews.

For my presentation as epiphany storyteller, I sat in a rocking chair and became Mary, the mother of our Savior. Around me were hundreds of woven baskets. They were decorated and plain. They were elaborate and useful. They were colorful. They were different in design. They were eye-catching and mind-blowing. They were props. They were the personal property of the women in attendance. The woven baskets held Mary's Memories. The memories were her "insider views": the real story of breathing, living, struggling women who had played upon the stages of the Bible's historical world. The baskets contained snippets, tidbits, and new insight from some strong, going-on sisters whose valor and dogged strength forced the patriarchs to put the sisters' names in our "official" canon of Scripture. The memory baskets provided us with several vivid portraits of Mary's visit with the wise women and reflections of other notable female characters from our spiritual journey!

Calling their names, even in a biased, often negative manner, signals their worth in the world. Mary Cartledge-Hayes, storyteller extraordinaire, has written an excellent tribute to even those whom we may label evil. Her book, *To Love Delilah*, further informs us that any woman who is named or referenced in the Bible needs to be researched for what her life can teach us. In the introduction she confesses,

> Thus, my earliest and strongest awareness of the rest of the Bible women was of failures: the evil, the irrational, the unfaithful. . . . Over time, I came to understand that the women of the Bible are largely single-issue characters. While many men get chapters, even books devoted to their stories, women's stories elicit a sentence or two. They are adjunct to the primary stories. Women appear long enough for someone to make a point and then disappear in a puff of smoke. . . . Our connection to them is tenuous, making them easy to stereotype, hardly worth the struggle to understand.

Seminary professor, sister, and friend, Emma Justes began my serious exploration into the lives of biblical women years ago. In one of my first pastoral care classes at Garrett-Evangelical Theological Seminary, she demanded that each person claim a biblical character who informed her life. She said, and I believe, "The Bible doesn't just speak to us; it speaks about us!" What a powerful revelation her words were to me! Off I went on a search to discover who I was in Holy Scripture. This journey continues today. As I read the stories of my biblical sisters, I do it with an eye and ear of seeing and hearing the other side of their stories. I know that their encounter with struggle, victimization, and pain forced them to act with self-determination and holy boldness. Their love for God pushed them to do the difficult and the different for survival of their posterity.

The Woman's Biblical Commentary has been an invaluable reference book while I've worked on this project. My conversations with sister-clergy, women's groups, and a diverse support group have provided insight, clarification, and additional views on what "might have been." I have become a biblical pundit! It is both my job and my joy to see these women of color in Scripture in a new light. I am charged with the awesome responsibility of bringing their plights, tensions, power of choice, and self-determination to bear on our contemporary lives. As I have read and reread their stories, they have whispered in my ear! As I have sat in prayerful meditation, they have come alive and led me to major discoveries. As I have asked them to share with me, other aspects of their lives have become startlingly clear. The girls want you to see them in your life! Like us, they have "been there and done that" and made it to the pages of the Book that guides our lives.

Myth has confined them to the stereotypes we hear again and again in sermons. The fables that were passed down and collected have been written with biased voices. We have learned to recite their stories with the same rote memory of a Mother Goose fairy tale! We won't go to the next level and push the story limits with "what else happened?" We have settled for the crumbs of their lives without looking for the whole loaf from which they fell! Yet with almost 1,200 names listed in Scripture and fewer than 150 of them female, we know there is much more for us to learn about the choices that allowed them to exercise self-determination for the sake of God's realm.

The collected tales of Mother Goose have nourished and nurtured us down through the years. These oral stories are familiar since they have been told and retold in most ethnic groups. They belong to the ages and bring joy as we hear them again and again. Each fairy tale has a teaching element to it. We find girls and women who are not as weak or insignificant as history often records. The women of Mother Goose teach us, through rhyme and reason, how to make choices that outsmart the "cunning ones." The sisters of Mother Goose will take on new meaning as they meet our biblical canon's Lady Wisdom, who was with God in the beginning of creation. In Proverbs 8, she gives us her version of the origin of the world. She watched and assisted in our careful and deliberate construction. She aided the Life Source in planting seeds of potential within us. She danced at the possibilities that lay before us. Today, she bids us come and join her in the dance. May these new stories help you feel her seismic rhythms and vibrations. May she call you to move with the powerful flow of the Spirit and leap into the dance of life with new vitality and intentionality.

As Mother Goose encounters Lady Wisdom, you will once again be reminded that each event of life carries us toward the grand conclusion of the whole matter of our life. Evil will be turned into good. Sorrow will be turned into gladness and joy. Defeat will be turned into victory. For we do not dance alone. The divine conspiracy of the Creator, Redeemer, and Sustainer encircles and dances with us to make myth, fables, and fairy tales become truth in action! Come on, join the dance!

May the brilliance of our collective epiphanies light your way, stir your spirit, and help you to select different options as you choose to exercise your self-determination. Choose this day to be different! Choose this day to become better! Choose this day to explore what makes you special and live your life to its full potential. Choose this day to let the wisdom of the ages encounter the myths, fables, and fairy tales that have controlled your life, and let them free you to live in the new millennium! Shalom, wise women!

THEY CALL HER LADY WISDOM!

They call her Lady Wisdom!
She runs unchecked throughout biblical literature
dancing, prancing, shouting out with glee,
"Come on, all you simple ones, have an affair with me!"

Wisdom, Come and Teach Us!

}⊣∤⊢∤

Tʜᴇʏ ᴄᴀʟʟ ʜᴇʀ Lady Wisdom! She tells another creation story. Her wise words are not merely suggestions or proposals. Her education is not to be ignored, debated, or taken lightly. She doesn't simply tell stories. She doesn't teach in parables. She offers us the proverbs of the ages, counsel that has been lived and passed down from generation to generation. She does not speak softly and hesitantly. She is not shy. Lady Wisdom boldly proclaims a powerful word. In Israel, Wisdom's counsel held the same authority as the word of the prophet, the priest, and the Torah.

The counsel of this sage is God. Humanity does not possess her. Lady Wisdom was before the beginning, and she belongs only to the Sovereign God. We are introduced to her in the first chapter of Proverbs. Compiled by Solomon, this collection of "wise teachings" is offered as instruction for living a godly life. Solomon, the wisest man in history, provides sound advice, passed down through the ages in poems, parables, quotations, and questions. Proverbs, Ecclesiastes, and the Song of Solomon are referred to as wisdom literature. Lady Wisdom is our instructor. Solomon informs us of Wisdom's gender in chapter 1, verse 20: "Wisdom calls aloud in the street; she raises her voice in the public square."

In Proverbs 8:22–31 she danced, she laughed, she rejoiced, and she played as God formed the world. She claims that she was in the council as humanity was formed. Can't you feel her excitement as God created? She watched while the foundations of the world were laid, as chaos and nothingness gave way to order and everything that we know. Wisdom was structured into the very fabric of creation. Yahweh's wisdom is evident as we ponder, with astute observation, the natural and social order of the universe.

Wisdom is the gentle yet firm voice of a knowledgeable parent. She is the collective counsel of the tradition of the elders. She is the prodding mother of King Lemuel. She is the valued wife, called the virtuous woman, in Proverbs 31. "Virtuous woman" in Hebrew is *Ishshah Chayil*, or a woman of strong force. She is a woman created by God. Yet we already know that Lady Wisdom runs the streets.

Can't you just see her as an offering; addressing men and women in their daily transactions in the public markets, on busy corners, and at the city gates? She is as accessible as any public person, and yet as elusive as the veiled women of the Middle East. Wisdom's message is not subtle, but direct: "How long will you simple fools be content with your simplicity? If only you would respond to my reproof, I would fill you with my spirit and make my precepts known to you" (Prov. 1:22).

Lady Wisdom is a prophet who pours out her heart calling us to God. She says without apology, "The fear of the Lord is the beginning of wisdom" (Prov. 1:7). The Hebrew word for "beginning" means the most important thing is this wisdom that comes from God. Wisdom defies usual categories. For Wisdom is not just some moral code or set of ethical principles. She is the work of the Ancient of Days. And her message is essential: "Get wisdom. Get understanding." She offers herself without price. All you need to obtain her is a desire.

Her persona as a worthy woman is noteworthy. Her main targets continue to be the young, inexperienced males who are tasting their first responsibility in public life. In the ancient clan structure of Israel, the father was the head of the household, but the mother had authority over the young children. Lady Wisdom is concerned that our inner motivation to do good and to protect the stability of the family continues. Even Jesus "grew in wisdom," we are reminded by the evangelist, Luke. Lady Wisdom is a guide. Lady Wisdom is a counselor. Lady Wisdom walks with her head held high and her direct voice calling.

Often we have heard of Wisdom from the last chapter of Proverbs with the timeless question, "Who can find a woman of virtue?" This chapter is a poem of praise that honors the attributes of the "ideal" woman. It's an artificially constructed section of material, called an acrostic in literature. Someone took the twenty-two letters of the Hebrew alphabet and, beginning with verse 10, used a different word to describe what qualities the "total woman" should possess. This method of teaching was good because it arranged the materials in a manner that would be easy to remember. Books were not common.

What is surprising is that this chapter begins with a woman's voice. A mother's prophecy is being transmitted to her son, who is the king. The man being addressed is called "Lemuel." We have no record of a king named Lemuel, but the name means "dedicated unto God." Scholars have determined that this material is addressed to an "ideal" king, by his "ideal" mother, about an "ideal" wife.

I find it interesting that in Hebrew Scripture we have a woman giving a prophecy or an oracle from God. Women were not valued. Women were not educated in the classical manner or taught in the local schools. Yet we discover a woman teaching her son through her own prophecy. Expositors have set forth the possibility that verses 10 to 31 of Proverbs 31 are a representation of the church of Christ, which is to stand as truth, purity, and an "ideal" influence in a world gone mad. The church is known as the "bride of Christ," and this would fit with that image.

It is unusual to have a *massa*, the Hebrew word for prophecy or inspired word of God, attributed to maternal counsel. However, Mother begins her instruction with an exhortation to chastity for her son: "Son, live a life of purity." Mother exhorts him to stay away from the commonly accepted low standards of his peers. She warns him against the evil influences of his day. She admonishes him to be righteous and just in his dealings with

others. She says that if he really desires an awesome sister for a wife, he needs to be above any condemnation himself. Sounds fair to me! No wonder wisdom is called a woman.

This woman, called Wisdom, knows that we need men who have godly principles in our lives. She understands that only an "ideal" man has the right to be on the lookout for a sister too good to be true. Who can find the "total" woman? It's an age-old question. Too often we try to access ancient wisdom using contemporary knowledge. You cannot go to *Webster's Third World Dictionary* to discover the Hebrew meaning for the word "virtuous." Remember, translated from Hebrew, the words "virtuous woman" are *Ishshah Chayil*, or woman of strong force. This doesn't sound like the "virtuous" women we hear preached about from our pulpits.

Women of strong force are everywhere we live. They have survived the continuous onslaughts of terror and tyranny. Women of strong force realize that they live solely dependent upon the strength and wisdom of God to face the challenges of life. Women of strong force have options to select from and recognize that to be challenged is a way of life. Women of strong force must be reckoned with as serious sisters. The woman, named Wisdom, sets some very high standards for determined women to follow.

As you look at the chapter outline, you become fully aware of Wisdom's competence, her self-definition, her mastery of many skills, and her ability to be in charge of various situations. Girl-friend is a vital entrepreneur, a wife, homemaker, mother, and employer-manager who takes care of business. Without the support of peers, without a network of mentors, and despite the fact that she is not considered noteworthy, the record stands that she is a woman of strong force!

I'm glad we have this composite picture of the women we have known, learned from, and around whom we have grown up. We each know women like the woman in Proverbs, chapter 31. Her life is our legacy. It's part of our heritage. She is one of the strong roots in our family tree. Women of color live lives full of challenge. We are women born of the union of tradition and crisis. Sorrow is the name of our mother. Suffering and

Striving are our aunts. Begin All Over Again is a grandmother to us all. We are the daughters, and our name is Wait! We stand at the crossroads.

We lived our lives under the whips, the lash, fire hoses, howling and growling dogs, and too often under the fists and the feet of the men in our lives. We lived our lives in bondage, often self-inflicted by our fantasies. We waited in the lush forest of Ethiopia, in the tropical wilds of Kenya, and in the palaces of Egypt. We waited through the forced exodus from Africa and during the voyage of many slave ships. We arrived on the shores of the land of the free and the home of the slaves in chains. We wait at the crossroads.

We waited in the seasoning pens, on the auction blocks, in the big houses and the shanties. We waited as we washed, cooked, cleaned, chopped, plowed, and hoed. We waited, embraced by loneliness, wrecked by pain and despair, kissed by poverty and misery, caressed by anxiety, fear, and disease. We wait still at the crossroads.

We pleaded and we hurt. We loved and have been loved for it in return. We had our bodies stolen. We have been traded, bartered, sold, abused, violated, raped, bred, exploited, married off, and taken advantage of, simply because of our color and our gender. We gave birth, and we suffered untold loss as we raised our babies and mammied theirs. We sheltered the orphan, welcomed the stranger, and embraced the lonely and unlovely. We have known the essence of despair. We stood crying as we waited in the throes of death. We have had parched throats as we thirsted for justice. Our feet were bloodied, cutting a path and making a way where there had been no ways, no means, and no money. Yes, we waited at the crossroads.

"Who can find a woman of strong force?" It's an insane question when you consider our history. Our mothers, our grandmothers, our aunts, and ourselves have been hungry while growing food for others. We waited in the fields and vineyards, picking fruit from trees, and sometimes, we watched our fathers and our brothers hanging as the strange fruit on those trees. We waited at the crossroads.

We watched our mothers grow old, doing the work of three. Up with the sun, working all day, seldom a kind word, and never equal pay. We watched our mothers step back and away from life; the system of poverty and oppression is a cruel teacher. We watched our mothers fade before our very eyes, wanting to live, but afraid. We waited at the crossroads.

We waited on the threshing floor at the cotton gin; at the lunch counters of the South; at the schoolhouse doors; and even at the doors of the house of God. For too many years we have been waiting. Yet Wisdom gives us a new tool to consider. She offers us an affair unlike any we have engaged in before. She pulls us from the despair of waiting. She teaches us that we have been seen and are valued. She recognizes our waiting. She affirms what we have achieved. She calls us women to be reckoned with, for we are the carriers and the pushers of our nation. Proverbs and this woman, named Wisdom, utter a prophecy declaring our time to be honored and praised. She upholds our right to be treated with dignity and with respect.

"Let her works praise her in the gates." Sisters, this is the word of God. It's a *massa*, an oracle, a prophecy, the inspired word of our God. We are worthy to receive double honor, for Wisdom decrees that "many women have done excellently, but you have surpassed them all." God says give us the fruit of our hands. Even though we have been denied, dejected, pushed back, and walked on, we waited, worked, and survived. It's our time to leave the crossroads. It's our time to move in a new direction. Wisdom is calling.

She calls us again: "It is time! I am yet seeking to pour out my spirit unto you. I want you to know my words . . . whoever will listen to me will dwell in safety, and shall be quiet from fear of evil" (Prov. 1:23, 33).

Listen. Listen. Lady Wisdom sounds like the voice of the Holy Spirit who danced on the Day of Pentecost, touching, kissing, being playful as she filled those disciples with fire and the power to be God's church. Who else but a woman named Wisdom would keep you waiting for forty days and come in without apology? Who else but a woman named Wisdom would prance in, wearing a swirling red dress, and turn the whole place up-side down, sending folks off in every direction into the world? My Lord, could this woman named Wisdom and the Holy Spirit be one and the same? Oh come, Lady Wisdom, reveal yourself to us again!

CAN WE TALK?

Isn't it exciting to read another version of the creation? Prov-erbs 8 is a version that speaks of a woman looking over God's shoulders; a woman watching with keen interest; a woman danc-ing, clapping her hands, and laughing as the biggest birthday party in the whole wide world was being prepared for human inhabitants. This version is not just one of information, but one filled with emotions and feelings of delight. Isn't this just like a woman?

This woman, named Wisdom, is known by every pastor. Wis-dom is even called "she" when referred to by the biggest chau-vinist! Yet there is little teaching on "her." She is the sage of the ancient past. She is the collective wisdom from many diverse and respected sources. She is a wild woman! She runs loose in the street, seeking those who will have an affair with her. Are you standing at a crossroads? Are you seeking new direction? This woman named Wisdom is right there with you. Want com-pany?

MOTHER GOOSE

Mother Goose lived with all her children,
unsupported by an elusive mate.
Through self-determination
she role-modeled independence for her daughters.
Birth control became a viable option!

Tales of Mother Goose

ᚼᚼ

"THIS WILL SOON BE OVER and then I can go home." Some of the most reassuring words in the Bible are found in Genesis 22:1 (KJV). The phrase "and it came to pass" implies that things will happen, situations will occur, circumstances do crop up, but time passes, and life goes on. Whatever situation you are in today does not have "the end" attached to it! God has a new scene prepared. God has a different stage set. God has an entirely different production prepared for your arrival. Things won't always be the same!

Revelation 12 details the story of a woman, pregnant with hopeful possibility, but in hiding. She's crying out in anguish while giving birth. And she's encountering a fierce assault from the one who stands prepared to devour her child. However, because of the great potential of the male child she is about to deliver, verse 6 declares, "The woman fled to the desert, to a place prepared for her by God, where she might be taken care of."

The book of Revelation is filled with signs and symbols. It's called an apocalyptic book, which means it reveals things that are to come. Nothing in it is to be taken literally, word for word. This is a book that requires reading, digesting, interpreting, and reinterpreting along the way. The only known fact about this book is that John, on the Isle of Patmos, had a vision and saw many marvelous and mysterious things.

I believe that the pregnant woman could have been Mother Eve, for God promised that her male seed, Jesus, would destroy the evil serpent by crushing his head (Gen. 3:15). Or this woman could be Mary, the mother of Jesus (Matt. 1:20–23). But since the mystery (who is the woman?) allows me entrance into its fold, I choose to believe that this woman could be any woman of color who has the potential to bring forth life!

I heard a sista-friend, Joyce Harris-Scott, deliver a sermon to a group of African American clergywomen in the United Methodist Church on this passage. She challenged us to come out of hiding and allow our individual and collective lights to shine as we minister to the places where we are appointed. Often our appointments are to "wilderness" places. Many times the buildings are antiquated, the former Anglo parishioners have fled, the endowments are spent, and the neighborhoods have changed. Joyce knows, firsthand, the struggle to have a healthy child (ministry) when all the evil forces of every system are working overtime to devour her energies, her possibilities, and her ministry! Yet Joyce declared that we have been protected by God until this, our time.

Her challenge remains with me. I've shared her message with several sisters around the country who have encountered fierce assaults as they labored to bring forth life. I especially remember Ava. She had been appointed to a "mission" church. This usually meant that the Conference would provide sustaining money for pastoral support, but there was little viability in the congregation or neighborhood. She worked diligently for four years making bricks without straw! She had a crazy male supervisor, who purposely left his fly open during their scheduled appointments. He was the type who would call her before dawn, as his wife slept, asking if he could come and pay a "pastoral visit." Finally, a new job opportunity arose several states away. She would be the associate pastor of an Anglo megachurch, with a huge salary increase and adjusted pastoral responsibilities. She thought it was time to give birth.

Ava is one of the most creative, colorful, and powerful women I've met. She is tall. She is dark skinned. She dresses in colorful ethnic garb. She is dynamic. She is passionate. She has charisma. She intimidated the poor "lil'" Anglo pastor who declared that he was simply "not ready" for her presence! In less than three months, he had trumped up charges against her and banned her from both "his pulpit" and the building! Needless to say, his supervisor, although female, was Anglo and racist. She suggested that Ava return home.

Ava listened to the voice of Wisdom: "Stay still in this desert place!" The situation gained much national attention. Several denominational groups had to be brought on board to assess the messy situation and to make recommendations to a bishop who was as racist as the pastor! It was a teachable moment to all involved. Racism is not a solo charge used to label individuals as "bad" or "evil." However, racism is white privilege, taken for granted and carried to damaging extremes. So several privileged white power brokers with the authority to squash emerging life felt that Ava was too intimidating, too forceful, too unlike them! She was drawing and coloring outside the lines. She had not been given their permission or blessings to get out of their limited vision box. Ava, like many other clergywomen of color, determined that she would give birth in the new place she'd been invited to do ministry.

The powers that be found her a home in an African American congregation, with "duties to be assigned." They hoped that she would simply disappear into the life of this congregation until the end of that appointment year and then go home. But when you are pregnant with life, no one can stop that baby from being born! God is involved. God has the plan. God knows when birthing is essential. God hid Ava in a cold, hostile environment so that the very best within her could be challenged. God took Ava from home, where there was a fierce assault, to a wilderness with an even more agonizing attack of evil! She spent many long days and sleepless nights, crying and in pain. As is the case with too many of us, she tried to figure out what she had done to cause these unwarranted onslaughts against her and her child. Yet she knew she could not run away. She came to understand that she was hidden within God's own powerful right hand. They could attempt to abort her pregnancy, but when God says "live," the birth will occur in spite of all the opposition!

Today, her baby is away from the denominational walls, yet she maintains ties with them! She runs a wellness ministry for the community called Colorful Threads. She gives life. She offers hope. She provides opportunities. She combines the best of the church with the best of nonprofit offerings, gathering folks who would never enter the sanctuary walls. Her ministry weaves together different strands of the arts and focuses on spiritual, mental, emotional, and physical wholeness. She advocates education in home ownership, history, tutoring, mentoring, and parental training. She has been supported by those who watched her stand tall despite the racism and sexism that sought to bring her down. She remained loving at a time when hatred and revenge could have been her choices. She refused to even file a grievance against the man who worked so diligently to destroy the life within her! She has given birth and is now stronger than ever. She has begun to thrive as she uses her self-determination and is the independent role model for other women who are pregnant with inner visions and struggling to discern how and where to give birth!

Joyce Harris-Scott was correct in her application of that passage from Revelation. God hid Ava away until the proper time and right place for birth to occur. We'd like to believe that the institutional church "wants to do the right thing." We hope that the day will come when racism and sexism will stop the multiple abortions performed on women in ministry. We pray for the day when we can stand tall and be counted as worthwhile contributors to God's church. However, believing, hoping, and praying won't necessarily make it so! God keeps hiding us in the most unlikely places. What Ava's story teaches us is that although we might be "hidden," God has not forgotten where we are! God prevents fierce assaults from killing us or our children. God allows the attacks to be visible and teachable moments for all around. And God uses these times to gather a "birthing community" around us.

Ava did not have the proper midwives around her at home. She was still considered a child herself! But in a new place, people watched to see what this powerful woman was going to produce. They saw her beauty. They respected her style. They enjoyed her new and different approach to Scripture, pastoral care, and community outreach. Those with experience to assist her were drawn to her. Those who had monetary resources, networking abilities, and fading dreams of their own joined her "birthing community.

When the battle got hot, folks from across the city and throughout the nation came to stand around and tell her when to pant and how to wait. They became pregnant with her. They helped her bear her labor pains. They were involved in the delivery!

It's essential that we have a birthing community. And it's essential that we know birth control methods! Not everywhere is a good place to be pregnant! Not all places are sterilized properly or conducive to helping the new infant thrive if it's born there. Sometimes we just need to know how to say "NO!" Sometimes we simply need to look at the options God places before us and risk moving away from home. All folks are not trained, equipped, or capable of being your midwife. Your child is too valuable to allow it to die before it lives, so God hides you until the circumstances are right.

The evil forces did not destroy Ava's life-giving abilities. As a matter of fact, their fierce attacks allowed God to show up and show out in a more visible and far-reaching manner than remaining within the confines of any local congregational building. The God of life both impregnated and empowered Ava's ability to bring forth gushing new vitality. Thanks be to God who continues to hide women until their proper time and place have come. Thanks be unto God for women who know when it's time to come out of hiding and to give birth to their very best selves!

CAN WE TALK?

Giving birth is more than simply having a biological child! The reality is that we all need to be pregnant and we each need to give birth to new ideas, visions, and dreams. Ava was not able to bear a biological infant. She knows the pain of many women who have longed for this pivotal experience. Yet she is a woman who has given birth to hopeful projects, inclusive ministries, and effective outreach that nurture and nourish the communities in which she lives.

Every year the world celebrates Advent. Every year the stage is set for the manger, animals, Wise Ones, and "The Family" to make their appearance. Yet we neglect remembering that Jesus can only be born each year if his mother is pregnant each year! So Advent really means Mary is pregnant! As we stand at the crossroads of a new millennium, the world is waiting for you and me to give birth to new life. Are you pregnant?

THREE LITTLE PIGS

Three little piglets went out to see the world.
The wolf thought he had them because they were merely girls!
One was greedy. One was lazy. The other had awesome intellect.
The wolf was had. The sisters were so glad that one of them
had more than common sense. She commanded R-E-S-P-E-C-T!

Armed and Dangerous

ᛏᛂᛏᛂᛏ

O NCE UPON A TIME, there lived three little piglets. They were born, bred, educated, and trained in the same house and in the same fashion. But one little piglet was lazy. One little piglet was greedy. And one little piglet was industrious, intelligent, and conscientious. Time passed, they grew up, and the time came for them to move out into the world on their own.

The lazy little piglet decided to build a house. The piglet wasn't concerned about having a firm foundation; she just wanted a place to party. In order to get finished so she could rest and get plenty of sleep, she built her house on shifting sand. The second little piglet began with a solid idea and even laid a solid foundation, but lunchtime came and a grumbling stomach hurried the little piglet along. Grabbing some sticks, which were close by, the greedy piglet completed her house and went to find some food. The third little piglet worked long and hard. Many hours of sweat and labor went into her planning. Little sleep and hurried eating kept this hard worker at her toil. Armed with an MBA and many wise contacts, she had the house custom designed to her exact specifications.

The first little piglet told her, "Sis, it doesn't take all of that." The second little piglet told her, "Girlfriend, you'd better slow down so that you can enjoy your life while you're young." But the third little piglet was determined to build a house that would stand through the years, keeping her and her posterity safe. Meanwhile, watching all of their building activities was their archenemy, the wolf. The wolf was always lurking in the wings, waiting for the right time to strike and to devour. "Surely this will be a piece of cake," he thought. "These are only girls!"

While the first little piglet snored deeply, tired and worn from a wonderful party, into her consciousness came the sound of a rushing wind. Huffing and puffing, the wolf was just outside her door. Now, she might have been a lazy piglet, but she wasn't a stupid piglet. Realizing that her home was not fortified well, she headed for the rear door. As the shifting sand gave way and the walls came tumbling down, the lazy little piglet ran to her second sister's house.

The first little piglet entered her sister's home and felt safe. Of course, the second little piglet felt superior. Then they had a feast and went to bed, well fed and feeling secure. The wolf was still waiting, plotting, and planning. While the two little piglets slumbered, the wolf was casing the second house, looking for unfortified places. Both sisters awoke to the sound of great anger. The wolf couldn't come through the foundation of cement, but he had found the stick-built structure easy to destroy. As the two little piglets went running to the wise sister's house, the wolf watched them, laughing, planning a huge barbecue feast.

But the third little piglet's house was fully fortified. It withstood the huffing and puffing as well as the angry winds of fury. The third little piglet's house stood solidly in spite of the cunning wolf's well-planned attack. With gratitude, the first piglet, Lazy, and the second piglet, Greedy, embraced with great appreciation the industrious, conscientious, and intelligent sister who had saved all of their lives in a home that was armed against the planned strategies of their enemy, the wolf.

In the fairy-tale version of the three little pigs, this is the end of the story. But there is no resolution with the wolf. We are left hanging as to where the wolf went or if the wolf's dangerous forays against little pigs continued. But, sisters, we can rest assured that the wolf did not simply lie down and die. Friends of mine, please know that the wolf did not just disappear off the face of the earth. Beloved, the wolf is alive and well. The wolf is yet waiting and watching, huffing and puffing, ever ready to blow our little house down. Our job is to be armed and dangerous whenever the wolf shows up. Dear ones, the wolf is stronger than ever before. The wolf is angrier than ever before. And the wolf is filled with more evil plans against the people of God than we can imagine.

The church age began at Pentecost, when more than three thousand souls were added to the membership in one day. But with progressive modernity, intellectual technology, and humanistic theology, we find ourselves in a day when the church of the living God is losing ground. Since we know that God has not abdicated the church, we can conclude that we are actively engaged in battle with our enemy, the huffing and puffing wolf.

Fanned by persecution, the gospel of Jesus Christ spread around the world, building faith communities and calling the people of God to care for the oppressed, downtrodden, poor, and neglected. Deacons were first selected and then consecrated to handle the public welfare cases. The church has always known its role until little pigs and piglets got both lazy and greedy and forgot about the ministry of missions. For the first time in sixty years, the evil, mean, and vicious spirit of greed has gained great popularity in the politics of the land of the free, home of the slave, while in God we trust!

The New Deal of President Roosevelt gave godly and compassionate consideration to the young, the elderly, and the poor, while the Sad Deal of President Clinton and Newt Gingrich has almost wiped out welfare, food stamps, summer jobs, Head Start, school lunches, Medicare, and Medicaid. If your congregation is still debating the issue of maintenance versus missions, I submit to you that the dilemma is a result of the huffing and the puffing of the wolf.

Our standards in the congregation of the righteous have fallen so low that most of us are afraid of preaching against domestic violence, child abuse, celibacy outside marriage, and the dangers of alcohol and recreational drugs because it will squarely hit so many of our officers and pledging members. When I was growing up, the church of God preached against a lack of morals. There was no question that shacking up, getting abortions, practicing homosexuality, imbibing strong drink, and engaging in illicit affairs, even between consenting adults, were sins. Now, on Sunday mornings, we might hear three meaningless points, concluded with a cute story that is not relevant to where we are hurting or where we are searching for answers. Today's church planners call it giving the paying customers what they want when really it's catering to the huffing and the puffing of the wolf.

I declare unto you that the times are evil. Violence is everywhere, regardless of where you live. We are surely living in mean times. Broken relationships, family members on drugs, and church cliques and splits bring battles with severe depression, suicide, and even homicide into our midst. The huffing and puffing of the wolf have not quieted, slowed, or stopped. But I thank God that we have an encouraging word from Holy Scripture in regard to this conniving wolf.

Paul writes to the church at Ephesus to encourage them in this warfare against evil, which is both cosmic and earthly. The main thrust of the book of Ephesians is the triumphant sovereignty of Jesus Christ and our unity in the family of God. In our struggle, Paul admonishes us to remain Christlike. We cannot resort to fighting evil with evil. We cannot fight against cosmic powers with intellect and acquired theological skills. No amount of hierarchical energies, assumed authority, or conferred control can win this war. This is a war that can be fought only with the battle gear of our Commander in Chief! "For we wrestle not against flesh and blood, but against powers, and principalities, and rulers of evil in high places" (Eph. 6:12).

I often wondered, "Where were the 'high places'?" I once believed that political systems and their leaders were the high places until I remembered that God sent Moses to confront the pharaoh, had Daniel ignore the king, and had Paul defy the Roman government. Political power is not a threat to God. The highest places where evil reigns are the pulpits! They're the places where the Word of God is to be proclaimed and uplifted. So Jesus warns us in Matthew 7:15–16: "Watch out for false prophets. They come to you in sheep's clothing, but inwardly they are ferocious wolves. By their fruit you will recognize them."

Friends, huffing and puffing is going on in the pulpits! Satan has an all-out campaign to destroy those who preach and those who practice truth!

This battle with the huffing and puffing of the wolf is not specifically against human beings. Our primary fight is against demonic influences. These powers are battling for control of our souls for all eternity. Our job is to proclaim, to hear, and to live the message. The good news is that, in the end, the people of God win. Read the end of the Book! And we win because we are dangerously armed with God's gifts of warfare.

Paul had firsthand knowledge of the wolf. Paul was imprisoned after many years of trials, troubles, and tribulations as an itinerant pastor. If anyone knew about recalcitrant church folks, it was Paul. If anyone knew about the heartache of unfulfilled, temporary relationships, it was Paul. If anyone knew about the betrayal and fickleness of those he came to help, it was Paul. If anyone knew about the difficulties of raising apportioned fees for the welfare of the poor, it was Paul. Facing death, knowing that he had fought a faithful fight, Paul wrote to encourage the church to stay united, to utilize every spiritual gift as resource, to maintain high ethical standards, and to reject popular pagan practices.

As he drew his letter to a close, he said,

> Finally, in conclusion, let me sum up all that is in my heart toward you. Finally, as my earthly life draws to an end, let me tell you how I have made it through these difficult years. If you don't remember any of my other messages, this is what you need to do: Be strong in the Lord and in the strength of God's power. Put on the whole armor of God, so that you may be able to stand against the tricks and snares of the devil. For our struggle is not against enemies of blood and flesh, but against the rulers, against the authorities, against the cosmic powers of this present age, against the spiritual forces of evil in the heavenly places. Therefore, since you know this, take up, put on, arm yourself with the whole armor of God, so that when the wolf comes you may be able to withstand, and having done everything you know to do, just stand. (Eph. 6:10–14; Peterson translation, *The Message*)

Paul said, "My head is facing a chopping block, but I realize that our power ultimately depends upon the infinite power of the living God who has armed us like warriors to win every battle." The basic equipment Paul outlines includes the *belt of truth*, since Satan fights with lies and half-truths. We have a *breastplate of righteous living*, since Satan attacks the heart, the seat of our emotions and self-esteem. There is the *helmet of salvation*, which keeps our faith strong when Satan comes to fill our minds with doubt. We are given a *shield of faith*, which protects us against the insults, defeats, failures, and temptations that come our way. And as God's warriors, we are provided with the Holy Spirit as a *sword of offense* against the enemy of our souls. And last, but not least, Paul wrote, we are to be armed with the *gift of prayer*: "Pray in the spirit on every occasion" (Eph. 6:18).

As an ambassador in chains, Paul says that when your armor has been penetrated, when the blows seem to be coming too fast and too furious, you can yet stand firm and pray. Prayer works. When we pray, God hears. When we pray, God intervenes. When we pray, things change; people change; we change. Paul says, "I hear the huffing and the puffing. I can even feel the wolf's warm breath on my neck, but I need you to pray for me so that I can be fearless as I continue to make known the mystery of this gospel message" (Eph. 6:19).

Dear ones, the solution to the huffing and puffing of the wolf is for you and me to be steadfast in prayer. Prayer gets the reinforcements of heaven sent on the run. Prayer is our backup, our fortification, and our strength for continued standing in the heat of battle. When it seems as though we can't fight anymore; when our war strategies have been plucked apart by the enemy; when the walls of our little houses have started to lean, to rattle, and to shake under the huffing and the puffing, Paul encourages us to pray.

We are to pray for one another. And we are to get others to pray for us as prayer partners, for the wolf never slumbers. Only prayer connects us to the One who watches over us without ceasing. We are to be alert in prayer. We are to persevere in prayer. We are to be in a constant attitude of prayer. The wolf is vicious. The wolf is relentless. The wolf is always on the attack. We need to remain in contact with the One who is on our side and can outsmart the wolf! We cannot do it alone. The good news is that we are not little pigs sent to fight by ourselves! And we need to remember that there are others in the army of God who are armed with prayer to see us through every satanic attack of the huffing and puffing wolf. We need to have active, ongoing prayer groups in every church.

I tell you, I'm so glad that I have friends who are prayer warriors; individuals who carry me to the throne on a daily basis. On those days when the way is rough, and the going is tough, and the hills are hard to climb; during those times when I've tried all I know, done all I could, played every trick, and used up every available strategy, I'm glad to know that somebody is praying for me.

In the church of my childhood the people of God used to request that others would "pray my strength in the Lord." I didn't understand it then. I thought it was just the formal ending of the testimonial liturgy. But I've come to discover that prayer strength is the only strength we can rely upon.

Chuck, Giraurd, and I moved to Michigan at the end of June. My only daughter followed in September. By October she was back on drugs, selling drugs, and engaged in every vile habit. We had to put her out of our home. She was homeless for many months. My heart felt like it was on a chopping block. The huffing and the puffing of the wolf had gotten to me, for it had attacked my child. There were days I couldn't pray, but others prayed for my strength in the Lord! I had no answers. And since I didn't know what else to do, I went to God in prayer.

I didn't have fancy words. I didn't try to use any printed theological formulas. I didn't have the energy to make up contrived statements to impress God. But I prayed simple words: "Lord, help." I prayed easy words: "Bless us, God." Sometimes my prayer was just the tears I shed; other times my prayers were the moans of my grieving spirit and the sighs of my broken heart. And very often it was plain "Jesus."

I talked to all the people I knew about Grian. If they were Christians, they were obligated to pray. Whenever someone asked me about her, I asked him or her to pray. Being ashamed to share your pain with others is the huffing and puffing of the wolf!

Ultimately, God controls the wolf. The wolf is at the door, but Jesus said, "I am the door" (John 10:9). Jesus went to Calvary to take control from the wolf. The huffing and the puffing continue, but the wolf has no teeth. Two months after my daughter left home, I preached in Little Rock, Arkansas, at the Hoover United Methodist Church. Who marched in with the choir? Who led the liturgical dance troupe in praise to the song "I Believe I Can Fly"? Who asked me to send her a Bible she could read because she's reading the Living Word every day? It was my daughter! The fervent and effective prayers of the righteous worked on our behalf.

Don't just take my word. Ask Lazarus, who had been captured by the huffing and puffing of death when prayer called him to live again. Don't just take my word. Ask the blind man sitting by the roadside, whose prayer was only a yell at Jesus. Don't just take my word. Ask the woman with the issue of blood, whose only prayer was to reach out and touch the hem of his garment. Regardless of the sounds of fury and anger all around you—it makes no difference how fierce the sounds and how ferocious the look of the fangs—the equipment of fervent and effectual prayer makes you armed and dangerous against every wolf. Finally, when you have done all you can, stand on prayer.

I encourage you to be a conscientious little piglet. Build your house on the sure foundation of 2 Chronicles 7:14. This promise of God declares, "If my people, called by my name, will humble themselves and pray, seek my face and turn from their wicked ways, then will I hear from heaven and forgive their sins and heal the land." Sisters, it's praying time. The wolf is at the door. The huffing and the puffing is loud in our homes, in the church, and even in our pulpits. The wolf is after our children. The wolf is after our relationships. The wolf is after our communities. The wolf is after us. And God wants us armed and dangerous! God wants us to pray. If justice is to reign, we have to pray. If the captives are to go free, we have to pray. If the battle is to be won against the cosmic powers of evil, we have to pray. For our God reigns. All power in heaven and earth is in God's hand. As Jesus rose to return to heaven, he left that power with us. So, little pigs, we have to wake up. We have to be more determined to spend private devotional time with God, prevailing in prayer. And we, like Paul, have to ask others to uphold us in their prayers. Only then can we be assured that we have a little "som'thin', som'thin'" to use against that ungodly critter, the wolf!

Once upon a time there were three little piglets who had to contend with a big, bad, huffing and puffing wolf! The wolf is yet alive and well. So which little piglet are you?

CAN WE TALK?

The issue is prayer and our use of this powerful resource. When you're standing at the crossroads, don't panic. Pray! When you're confused, unnerved, and fearful of what's ahead, pray! For prayer connects us with God. Prayer dispatches help from the realms of glory. Prayer is essential for discerning direction at life's crossroads.

Prayer is more than cute, pious-sounding sentences employing "thee" and "thou" and other antiquated words we've learned from King James! Prayer is essentially an attitude of being dependent upon the Ancient of Days. Prayer is an internal yielding and submitting to the will and way of God, who has ordered our steps. Prayer is a striving to hear the inaudible, to see the invisible, and to become more in touch with the mysterious whom we call God.

Standing at the crossroads? Don't get frantic and run down that old familiar path of repetition. Instead, get still. Let Granny's prayer song begin to rise in your spirit: "Creator, I stretch my hands to thee. No other help I know. If thou withdraw thyself from me, where else can I go?" And even as the tears of helplessness begin to fall, know you're engaged in the powerful act of prayer.

Ebony Black and the Pygmies

"Call for the midwives; let them kill the boys," they said.
"Good as done!" was the reply they heard ringing in their heads.
Why, they were men. They were in charge. No question their
demands would be followed. They give the orders,
then carry them out.
The dilemma is solved without problem.
Well, they forgot that a birthing God was in the plan.
With subservient women and passive resistance,
pygmies were made of those "big men"!

Dedicated to my United Methodist Women sisterhood

It Takes a Woman to
Raise the Village!

⊦⊣⊦⊣

O PRAH WINFREY'S MADE-FOR-TELEVISION MOVIE *The Women of Brewster Place* was based on a book by Gloria Naylor. The book begins with the telling of some very basic facts that are unknown by the people who live in this little village community. You need to understand that Brewster Place was the brainchild of several clandestine meetings of a group of rich, powerful, and greedy men. They came together, propositioned each other, bargained with each other, and slowly worked out the very best financial consummation of their respective political desires. In a damp, smoke-filled room, filled with men who considered themselves to be "in charge," the little village of Brewster Place was conceived. Three months later, with its illegitimate conception hidden from the general public, it was given birth by the "founding fathers." Two years later, the whole community turned out for the baptism of this misbegotten child. As one of the founding fathers smashed a champagne bottle against the building to christen it, he declared that the community was now making space for those patriotic "boys" and their families who were returning home from the Great War.

There was a sense of hope and promise as immigrants hurried to occupy a new boulevard that the founding fathers said was destined to become a new, major part of the business district. So no one complained when several auxiliary streets were closed down. No one spoke up when a six-foot-high wall was erected to control traffic. There was no opposition when the founding fathers said that an exit for Brewster Place would happen in the near future. There was no one to fight for these newcomers who had no political influence. These were people who were mellow skinned, spoke in different languages, and ate strange-smelling foods. When Brewster Place became a dead-end street, it also became a dead project. The wall became a fixture on Brewster Place. It soon appeared foolish to question its existence. It just was.

Sisters, it's part of our human nature to erect walls. For walls are those great, impenetrable, and perplexing barriers that serve to keep "them" away from "us." All of us have difficulty relating to those who are unlike us or abnormal. "They" are not worthy of living on our side or being in our place along with us. "They" don't measure up to our standards. "They" are not like us in appearance, in economic status, in cultural heritage, or in religious belief. Too many of "them" around "us" becomes a very real threat, so we begin to find some methods of building walls, maintaining barriers, and keeping "them" in their place. Division and disunity begin when we decide that we are better than or superior to "them." Division and disunity are insidious and operate on many levels. They are subtle and start with the simple act of wanting to narrow the range in which others might move and operate. The damage done by division and disunity is often not apparent since it appears as if we simply want to keep "those of us who are alike" together. So, really, we don't build walls to keep them out; we just erect barriers to close ourselves in.

For the good of all creation, God has called forth women, in all times and in all places, to be the ones to tear down walls. It makes no difference where division and disunity are conceived; God has a history and a habit of calling forth women who will unite and bring down walls. Before the beginning, God decreed that it would take women to erect villages and nurture creation. The Bible declares that Eve was the mother of us all, and mothers want their families to stay together for the common good.

So, women, with our creative abilities and nurturing instincts, we will devise strategies to tear down walls!

United women who erect villages and save lives, while protecting male leadership, are nothing new. United women, with a method of linking hands to raise up the downtrodden and to manipulate the political powers, are as old as the biblical record. United women, with a method of saving children, assisting other women, and downplaying their collective wisdom, strength, courage, and inner power, are wise women we need to uplift. We've been "legitimate" feminists or womanists only *a few short years*, but we've been birthing, nurturing, and saving lives since the world began!

The story recorded in the book of Exodus is a tribute to the legend of united women saving lives. This story is about the enslavement of the Israelites in Egypt. It recalls their journey in the wilderness. It sets a stage in their history when their growth in numbers necessitated the development of new laws and new leadership. The Exodus story is like the story of Brewster Place. In the hushed political courts of the pharaoh, a plot was established to destroy the people of God; a people who were different from the majority culture. On literal and metaphorical levels, the Exodus narrative relates how an evil plan was devised to make the people of God powerless. The story opens with the intervention, the ingenuity, and the united power of women. Exodus is really a story about how five women— Shiphrah, Puah, Jocabed, Miriam, and Pharaoh's daughter— linked hands to help the nation of Israel survive. Exodus is the story of how five women united to help Israel move from severe oppression to freedom and self-determination. Exodus is the story of how five women made male leadership and, eventually, the Exodus possible! I declare unto you today, my sisters, that it really does take a woman to raise a village! And the Bible tells us so!

It is believed that Moses must have recorded these events around 1450–1410 B.C.E. because it was in the Nile valley that papyrus was formed. This story is set in Egypt where God's people had been brought by Joseph to be saved from starvation. But Joseph died, and all that he did to save both the Egyptians and the Israelites from starvation was forgotten. A new pharaoh had arisen in the land. He saw the rapid growth of the Israelites, who were different. So he began to plot their destruction. His plan is recorded in Exodus 1:9: "'Look,' he said to his people, 'the Israelites have become much too numerous for us. We must deal shrewdly with them or they will become even more numerous, and if war breaks out, they will join with our enemies, fight against us, and leave the country.'" So, his number one plan was to enslave them.

The Bible says that the more oppressed the Israelites became, the more they multiplied. As Christians, we already know that our trials come only to make us strong. And if we never had a problem, we'd never know that God could solve them, and we'd never know what trust and faith in God could do. Plan number one didn't accomplish Pharaoh's desired end. So, plan number two was to make their lives bitter by working them ruthlessly with backbreaking slave-labor. Through it all, the Israelites continued to trust in God. Pharaoh did not understand that trials, temptations, and troubles create "overcomers." Pharaoh's second plan failed.

Finally, in desperation, Pharaoh's third plan was to kill all the male infants. If you kill the males, the babies will stop being produced. If you kill the males, the growth of the nation will cease. If you kill the males, the threat to "us" will be over. Plan number three brings us to Exodus 1:15, when two women, Shiphrah and Puah, are called before Pharaoh. You know these sisters are important because they are named! These are not just "certain women"; these are not some nameless, faceless, insignificant women. There are fewer than 150 females named in all the biblical records, and these sisters have significant names. Now, Pharaoh believed that he was almighty, all-powerful, and in charge, so he dared to call in these women to help carry out his plan of death. But the name Shiphrah means "joy of parent." The name Puah means "one who will procreate." Pharaoh felt that women were insignificant, of little importance, and invaluable, yet he called for these midwives to carry out his decree. His instructions are in verse 16: "When you go to assist the Hebrew women in childbirth upon the delivery stool, if it is a boy, kill him. If it is a nonthreatening and worthless girl, let her live." Boyfriend didn't have a clue. This ignorant man ordered these women to commit murder, but they were committed to God's plan of life. When Pharaoh desired death, these women were determined in their hearts to provide unauthorized leadership through their silent acts of intervention. Not daring to talk back and having better sense than to be outright with their defiance, they were wise enough not to be openly rebellious. These sisters show us how those who are accorded secondary status and excluded from the circles of power were the very ones that the God of Glory utilized to be the unproclaimed sheroes and giants in the land.

Yes, the central human figure in the Exodus narrative is Moses, the Deliverer. However, Moses is not simply an exemplar for the Israelites; he is a type of Jesus. Moses is a symbol of the Coming One. Moses represents how the world is going to be won for God in spite of evil prevailing in the high courts of the land. And Moses could not have accomplished his role in history without the direct involvement, personal intervention, and countercultural interference of women because it takes a woman to raise and nurture creation!

This story of birth serves as a metaphor of liberation, for birth is explicitly a female expression of divine power. These female midwives initiated resistance against Pharaoh's plan of death, which would have included Moses. The very emergence of the people from confinement in Egypt occurs through another dramatic image of birth as the waters of the Red Sea part to allow the Israelites safe passage into freedom. Moses is able to record this story only because he and his people were enfolded in the amniotic fluids of God's miraculous mercy and delivered by way of the oceanic origins of amazing grace displayed by women.

In addition to Shiphrah and Puah, there are many other women associated with the life-giving waters in the Exodus story. We have to name Jochebed, Moses' mother, who carried him in her womb and determined to hide him in the tall reeds of water after she delivered him. Then we must name his sister, Miriam, who first appears as a sentinel, standing watch and protecting him from the banks of the river. This same woman, as priest, leads the nation of Israel in celebration when they cross the Red Sea. Then there is Pharaoh's daughter, a nameless foreigner, whom God pulls into this scenario of life bursting forth from the womb of water. She not only picks the baby up, but names him Moses, which means "drawn from the water"! This nameless African woman allows him to be nursed and taught at the breast of his own Hebrew mother. And this nameless African woman takes him into the very palace of the one who plotted to kill him in the first place. In her home, Moses is taught the principles and strategies of leadership. Finally, there is the wife of Moses, Zipporah. We meet her in Exodus 2. She and her sisters, all daughters of Reuel, the Midianite priest, meet Moses by the side of an old well. Water and birth. Water and concealment. Water and salvation. Water and deliverance. Water and love. Water and women. It takes a woman to erect the village and to nurture God's creation.

Throughout the book of Exodus, the omnipotence and omnipresence of God are emphasized through women who have always appeared to be unimportant and labeled as insignificant. But with unauthorized leadership, with acts of divine intervention, and with the innate wisdom of God, we are given a full picture of how God has always utilized the work of women to bring deliverance, salvation, and liberation. This biblical text provides us with a framework of unqualified advocacy for the oppressed, the different, and the powerless. Liberation theology has an understanding of the centrality of God's divine concern for the last and the least. It's part of God's divine plan for women to practice birthing strategies, tear down walls, erect safe villages, and nurture all of creation.

If Susanna Wesley had not thrown her apron over her head to pray in the midst of raising children in a manse where there was seldom enough of anything, the Methodist Episcopal, Christian Methodist, Free Methodist, United Methodist, African Methodist, or any other type of Wesleyan Church would not exist. Her steadfast faith in God gave her the wisdom to rear John and Charles Wesley. It takes a woman to raise a village!

Without the many unnamed women who took notice of the plight of little children being neglected and mistreated, where would we be? Without unnamed women rebelling against working mothers and children being exploited by ruthless entrepreneurs, where would we be? Without this collective force there would never have gone out a call for women to begin to set aside both their pennies and their prayer power, which formed the first women's societies, missionary circles, or the Temperance Society. Without the power of God calling an unrecognized African woman named Theressa Hoover, there would not be the politically astute and economically sound movers and shakers now known as United Methodist Women who stand more than one million strong and manage one of the strongest financial portfolios in the United States. Erecting a village requires all willing hands, regardless of their age or station in life.

Every mainline denomination is in serious trouble. There is yet a satanic plan to kill good leadership, regardless of gender, race, color, or creed. There is yet a strategy underfoot to keep us separated, divided, and living on dead-end streets. There is a method in leadership that effectively keeps the church from being all that God desires us to be. We are oppressed by separatist, classist, racist, and sexist plots. The plan is to destroy the people of God, but the waters are troubled. The birthing pains are growing stronger and more persistent. There is a loud call for women with helping hands to sign up for this war. God is calling for tired, overworked hands. God is calling for young, unskilled hands. God is calling for every hand that is willing to carry out any assignment, for it's a small piece of the much bigger plan. God is always bringing forth new life. God is yet participating in new birth. God is determined that there will be not only life, but abundant life. That's why Mary gave birth to Jesus. That's why women went to prepare his body and found out that he had burst forth from the womb of death. That's why it was a woman who was charged to "go and tell"! Without a woman there is no village!

Of course, God's call to the midwives brought them great personal chaos. But God paid great benefits by giving them both land and families. God's call to Jochebed brought her a new determination to defy the laws of the land, but God stepped in with salvation for her baby. God's call to Miriam demanded that she stand ready and willing to do whatever was required to save the life of God's Deliverer. And God made her a leader because of her faithfulness. God's call to a foreign woman brought her into contact with folks who didn't look like her, believe as she did, or have what she had. God used her to name Moses and to train him for the leadership role he was to play. It's always been the willing hands of women who defy the so-called powers and who bring life into the midst of death. It's women who continue to pull male leadership out of murky waters. It's godly women who stand, watching, waiting, and actively looking for ways to connect resources with needy people. God is still calling women to lend their hands and help erect and shape deliverance in the village!

A woman was raped at the wall that enclosed Brewster Place. When she came to herself, she saw an old, innocent drunk man who had fallen down by the wall. She took a brick from the wall and beat him to death. His innocent blood bathed the wall. Her rape and his death brought new life and new determination to the women of Brewster Place. A week after the drunk's funeral, the women decided to have a community street party. They got together to play, to sell home-baked foods, and to allow the children to have some fun. In the midst of the fun and forced gaiety, rain waters begin to fall.

A little two year-old-girl was playing and stumbled against the wall. When her mother heard her crying and got to the wall, there was blood on her baby's hand. This mother got hysterical. She began to yell and to scream. The other women came running to help. They came with bats, long barbecue forks, high-heeled shoes, and fingernail files. They came prepared to fight, armed and ready to attack the enemy. The enemy was the wall! And with instruments of destruction in their hands, they tore down the wall that had separated Brewster Place from the rest of the world. As they worked, united with helping hands, they sang.

When the people of the sixties tore down the walls of segregation, they sang "We Shall Overcome." When Lech Walesa and the Polish people tore down the walls of communism, they sang "We Shall Overcome." This story can be used for annual Women's Day celebrations across the world! The many diverse and helpful hands of women have made the church a strong, powerful, and viable force for life in the plan of God. I just believe that we, the women, have been mandated to erect every village and to tear down every wall. Deep in my heart, I just believe that with the call of God, the salvation of Jesus Christ, and the assorted gifts of the Holy Spirit among us, we are going to tear down the walls that divide God's church. God has given women the right, the ability, and the privilege of birthing forth liberation, reconciliation, and new life for all of God's creation. It takes a woman to raise every village! And, Sistagirl, God wants to use your willing hands!

CAN WE TALK?

Take a look at your hands. They are not just digits and palms attached to wrists. They are instruments of God, loaned to you to play your few chords in the symphony of the world. All of us are allowed a note or two. Your hands are valuable gifts.

Think of all you do with your hands. As we age, they help us get out of bed in the morning. They turn on the water we use to wash our faces and brush our teeth. They pull the coffeemaker out for us and fill the juice glass. They enfold others into our welcoming arms and, when necessary, wash little dirty behinds. Our hands load washers, hold mops and brooms to clean, wipe little snotty noses and even our own brimming tears. They work with us and for us. Our hands rock cradles and rule worlds!

It makes no difference whether our hands are manicured or not, the nails are sculptured or bitten ragged, our hands run the world. We clean the houses, type the letters, answer the phones, and point the way for those who think they are in charge! And you don't just have use of your one pair of hands. Our hands are connected around the universe. Women in Canada reach out to women in Australia. Those in China touch those in Africa. We uplift and uphold each other.

Standing at a crossroads? Reach out for a sister's hand!

BIG BO PEEP HAS LOST HER SHEEP — SHE ATE THEM!

Big Bo Peep got tired of watching sheep.
There were other options that lay before her.
So she made a feast of all those sheep
and opened a shop to sell wool!

The Art of Taking Low!

}⊣}⊢{

CHUCK AND I WANTED TO SEE *Amistad*, but the movie was sold out. We had a baby-sitter for Giraurd and decided we were going to see something on our evening alone. So we went to see *Titanic*. I knew that the movie was based on a historical cruise ship the builders had bragged even God could not sink. I also knew that God allowed an iceberg to show folks who is in charge. Even though it was not my first choice, we sat back to endure the retelling of the story.

It was a master love story. And if there is something I really enjoy, it's a good love story. The leading man was a poor, independent chap whose gambling won him a ticket in the steerage compartment of the ship. He was just glad to be going home. The leading lady was being peddled off by her mother to a wealthy man because her father had lost all of their money and then died. It was my type of story, where the underdog rises to the top. Of course, the wealthy man cannot believe that some dirt-poor chap could actually steal the leading lady away from him. When it happens, the wealthy man sets up the poor chap, accusing him of burglary, and has him arrested. Of course, "true love" wins out.

The poor young man is locked in the captain's quarters as the ship begins to fill with water. In my favorite scene the leading lady rescues him, and they swim back to the top deck of the ship. The rich man sees them together and comes to grab her away from the man she now loves. He shows her a pocket filled with money with which he proposes to buy her a seat on a lifeboat. She refuses his invitation. The rich man then makes some belittling remark about both her and the poor man. Then my favorite part of the scene occurs. This demure and petite woman stands back, sucks in her stomach, and hawks, spitting right in the rich man's face! Talk about gross! It was worth the price of both our tickets to me!

For a minute I remembered Mama. When something got on her last nerve, when she had just about reached the end of her patience and was past worn to a frazzle, her favorite saying used to be, "I'm so mad till I could just hawk and spit!" When I saw hawking and spitting on the wide screen, Mama lived again!

I know it sounds gross, and it looked as bad as it sounds. I pray I haven't offended your delicate sensibilities, but the girl was alright with me! I know that there are days when people will make you want to hawk and spit! (Or even do worse things to them!) People will get on your nerves. People will mess with you. People will jack you up. People will dust you off. People will leave you high and dry. People will say strange things. People will act real funny. People will disappoint you and let you down. And there are times when people will make you want to hawk and spit.

I work with crazy people all week long. There are those who will get under my skin. There are those wonderful people who drink too much and then come to work. There are those folks who have children missing curfew, get caught up in drugs, deal with abusive spouses, and then want to take it out on you! I attend worship with these same people. There are those in attendance who awake to the thundering silence of solitude and depression and simply want to find some method of fighting the feelings. There are those who are so close to the edge that you can see the sparks flying all around them. When these types go into action, they make you want to hawk and spit.

Perhaps you don't understand folks with personality types like mine. I have a razor-edge temper and a scissor-sharp tongue.

Jesus is working on me and in me, and I'm getting better day by day. But I haven't gotten above the daily push and shove of the world that continues to try to run me over. And if the truth be told, you haven't either! Regardless of how deep and Spirit-filled we are, there is no insulation from dealing with crazy folks, including those who live in your house and within you! It is no secret that when that woman spit, she spit for me!

I have a thirty-something-year-old son who is saved, good-looking, college educated, and gets on my reserve nerve. He has diabetes and refuses to do the right things. On my last two-and-one-half-hour trip to visit him during an emergency hospitalization, I inquired about what had happened. When he told me that he had been "forced" to eat some spicy fajitas and chocolate cookies, I wanted to hawk and spit! Then there is one of my sisters, whom I dearly love. Sista Riene came to help us out by watching Giraurd for a week while we got away. We had no problem with paying her a week's salary for her kindness. But when she walked in our door and handed me a bill for a car rental, I wanted to hawk and spit. But, wait, let me talk about the man I love. When I said something to Chuck about him "thinking he knows everything," he responded, "If I don't know it, it doesn't need to be known." I wanted to hawk and spit!

Hawking and spitting is just a metaphor for wanting to beat up on something when it seems that everything else in life is ganging up on you. There is a general sense of powerlessness that many of us feel these days. There are those days when nothing will respond correctly or appropriately. You can't control the spouse or significant other. You can't find a spouse or significant other. You can't control the kids you dress and feed. You can't manage to get the man and the marriage, or you just can't conceive a child. You can't control the power brokers who dictate how you work and what you're paid. Or you can't control the people you pay to work for you. It can get so bad that you can't even control your own feelings of depression, despair, and grief. The only thing that many of us feel we have control over is the automobile, so we get behind the wheels of our cars and all of our frustrations boil up and over. Too many of us act out our inner hostilities and anxieties through road rage. So hawking and spitting is fairly mild in comparison!

Abigail is a biblical sister who knows our feelings. She can teach us much about how to deal with our inner rages, our messed-up relationships, our boiling frustrations, and our desire to hawk and spit in somebody's face. Girlfriend walks on level ground with us, and I know her story is told to teach us godly principles for dealing with normal human anger. This woman was married to a certified fool, and her story is found in the twenty-fifth chapter of First Samuel. She is part of King David's history and, therefore, in the history of Christ.

David and his soldiers were running from a crazed King Saul. They were in the fields of a wealthy man named Nabal. As they camped out, they also watched the borders of his property. They were there when sheep-shearing time approached, customarily a festive occasion when all kinds of food and drink were made available and merrymaking took place. So David asked Nabal to send some of the prepared foods to him and his men in the field. He asked in a kind manner, "Be favorable toward my young men, since we come at a festive time. Please give your servants and your son, David, whatever you can find for them" (1 Sam. 25:8). Nabal refused. David didn't want to hawk and spit. He swore to kill Nabal and every male in the surrounding area! As he left for the battle, he took four hundred men with him to assuage his anger.

One of Nabal's servants got wind of the approaching danger and ran straight to Abigail. When she got the news, it is recorded, "Abigail wasted no time. She took two hundred loaves of bread, two skins of wine, five dressed sheep, roasted grain, raisins, cakes of figs, loaded on donkeys" (v. 18).

Lesson one from Abigail is to quickly acknowledge a threat. Too many of us live in denial. We don't want to see the danger that is right in our faces. We want to stick to our fantasy instead of facing what we need to deal with in a forthright manner. She lost no time in addressing the situation at hand.

Lesson two is that she prepared herself to confront David. She said to her servant, "Go on ahead. I'll follow you" (v. 19).

The Bible records, "But she did not tell her husband Nabal." Not everybody will help you get an issue cleared up. Nabal was the reason for the impending danger. She took matters into her own hands.

Abigail was a quick study in advice given by Jesus: "Agree with your adversary quickly" (Matt. 5:25). Lesson three is what Granny used to call the art of taking low. She tried to help me understand that you don't need to try and outtalk, outsmart, or outmouth everybody. Some battles are best won when we take low. This is not easy. This is not ego-stroking. This does not seem to be a position of power. However, I've come to understand that when we "take low," God will take the situation up! God is obligated to get revenge for us. It's a promise. "Vengeance is mine, says God. I will take care of them!" (Rom. 12:19). But as long as we want to "handle it," God can step back, fold those helping hands, and say, "You go, Girl." Sista Abigail decided to take low.

"When Abigail saw David, she quickly got off her donkey and bowed down before David with her face to the ground. She fell at his feet and said, 'My lord, let the blame be on me alone. Please let your servant speak to you; hear what your servant has to say . . . pay no attention to that wicked man Nabal. He is just like his name and his name is Fool'" (1 Sam. 25:23–25). Nabal might have been a fool, but Abigail surely wasn't.

Lesson four is to take responsibility for your part in any given situation. Don't lie. Don't take stuff that is not rightfully yours. Don't try to cover for another guilty party. Do take responsibility for what might be your part. Abigail was married to Nabal. We know, due to the custom of her day, that she didn't choose him; he was chosen for her. Nevertheless, she was partly responsible for whatever he did or did not do. Therefore, she met David with words of obligation upon her lips: "Let the blame be on me."

This is a difficult lesson for those of us who have grown up hearing more words of blame than of taking responsibility in our homes. This is not what we have learned at the dinner table where we seldom heard our parents ask for pardon or forgiveness. This is not part of the repertoire of actions that we fall back on immediately when confronted with conflict. But it's a lesson we can learn. When someone calls me brash, I can easily say, "Yes, there are many occasions when I am brash." When Chuck dares to call something I did or said "dumb," I can agree, "There are many areas in life where I am not knowledgeable." It makes no difference how ugly or unflattering the comment about me might be, there is something in it that I can "own." You will be shocked at how quickly your "owning" actions can stop arguments. Some folks are waiting for you to get defensive or angry. When you agree quickly with them, they are taken aback, and often you get the upper hand because they don't know how to respond! It was not Abigail's fault that David was on a murder mission, but she took part in Nabal's foolishness. Then she allowed David to become her instructor. She said, "I did not see the men my master sent" (v. 25). There are often things that hurt or offend others that we don't see. In the quiet of the moment, let them teach you. Be quiet, and learn something about yourself!

In the midst of most of our angry exchanges with others there is a blind spot somewhere. Someone has gotten a wrong message. Something has been misunderstood. Things could be projected onto us that we don't rightly deserve. Or there could have been some other unpleasant exchange that was not resolved, but covered over. These things always come back to haunt us. So this time, Abigail teaches us: don't gloss over mess. She is doing a good job of resolving this conflict before lives are lost.

Lesson five: Abigail became a bridge-builder and a peacemaker when she said, "Let no wrongdoing be found in you as long as you live . . . my master will not have on his conscience the staggering burden of needless bloodshed or of having avenged himself. . . . May you be blessed for your good judgment" (vv. 28–32). This woman was determined that no blood would be shed, so she took it upon herself to resolve the conflict. Not only did she bring something good to eat, she spoke words of kindness that resounded within David's heart. "Then David accepted from her hand what she had brought him and said, 'Go home in peace. I have heard your words and granted your request'" (v. 35). The war was over before it began. Innocent lives were spared. Conflict resolution worked well.

Of course when Abigail returned home, she found Nabal partying and drunk, so she had to leave the matter alone! This is the sixth and final lesson she teaches us. When it's over, let it go! She realized that Nabal's cookie dough was not well baked. She understood that his elevator did not rise to the penthouse floor. She left well enough alone. The matter was settled. She let it go. We like to hold on, chew on it, drag it through more mud, dredge it up again and again, and stew in it till it's dog meat. We must learn how to move on ahead. And we can't move until we learn to let go of even today's junk.

Matthew 6 details the Lord's Prayer that we learned as children. But we stopped learning too soon. This particular prayer does not conclude the way we have commonly been taught. It goes on and says, "If you forgive those who sin against you, then God will forgive you. But if you do not forgive others their sins against you, God will not forgive you." This is a hard saying. But it's in the Book. We need to read it with understanding. What it boils down to is this: we receive the forgiveness that we give! This is why it is ultimately important that we learn how to let go and move on. God has such an accurate accounting ledger that nothing will be forgotten or overlooked. We don't have to hold the records. We don't have to keep score. We can move on. Abigail did and look what it got her.

When Nabal sobered up, she told him what had happened: "His heart failed him . . . about ten days later, the Lord struck Nabal and he died" (vv. 37–38), and "then David sent word to Abigail asking her to become his wife" (v. 39). And she did!

CAN WE TALK?

For those of us raised in the United States, it is difficult to take low! We have been taught to "take charge." We have been taught to "kick tail and take names." We have learned well how to "do in others before they can do it to us"! And yet Abigail shows us a tried-and-true method of resolving conflict. It's not a popular way of conducting oneself in a cruel world. It's not an ego-stroking manner for those of us who have been wounded time after time. It's not even an approach that makes us feel good! Yet it's an alternative way of behavior that gets God's attention and involvement!

Got a situation that is really giving you the blues? Reread Abigail's strategies and try them on for just this particular occasion! They're guaranteed to work.

Tamar — Codependent No More!

Cinderfella, Cinderfella, treated like a slave.
She served the mean ones very well until the day
Queen she was made.
Guess who's sorry now?

The Girl's Alright
with Me

}⊣{⊢{

"THE GIRL'S ALRIGHT WITH ME," sang the Temptations in the sixties. These very same words had to be said by Judah about his daughter-in-law, who took advantage of his need for sex and won her place in Israel's history. When Judah tried to play Lil' Sista, she held on. When Judah denied her, she went right on ahead with life. Even after Judah impregnated her and took advantage of her position, she did not give up. And even when she was mistreated and sent away like last week's trash, she refused to back up and quit. One day, Tamar stood at the crossroads. She took a risk. It almost cost her life. But the girl's alright with me!

Tamar comes on the biblical scene in Joseph's narrative. Judah, Joseph's older brother, is the one who steps in and prevents Joseph's physical death by taking Joseph out of the pit and selling him to a band of Egyptians. So, in some ways, Judah is a minor portrait of a deliverer. But Judah is also a schemer and a liar. The canon records this story of family denial, betrayal, and deceit. It's the story of a dysfunctional family at its worst. And that's not new either! Judah marries a Canaanite woman, Bathshua, and has three sons. Since names are always powerful indicators of lifestyles to come, we find Judah with an eldest son, Er, which means "exposed"; the middle child, or "knee baby," who is named Onan, which means "vigorous"; and the youngest son, Shelah, whose name means "quiet."

By this family a woman is found, whose name is Tamar. We don't know if she's Israelite or Canaanite. We just discover that she is found suitable for the oldest son, Er, but his lifestyle is "exposed" to God, who doesn't like it, and Er dies. There was in Israel's understanding the levirate obligation to be honored. This meant that since a woman was only property and could not inherit wealth, if a man died without a male heir, the next brother had to have a son with her so the wealth could be passed along family lines. So, it was right, proper, and fitting that Brother Onan take responsibility for making a son for his dead brother, Er.

We are not told what Tamar looks like. She may have been beautiful. She may have been an ugly old soul. What we know is that Onan had sex with her, as was his right and obligation. But instead of impregnating Sista, he practiced the birth control method called withdrawal before ejaculation. God was not happy with his actions, and Brother Onan died. This leaves the head of the clan, Judah, in distress. Two of his three sons are dead. He has one son left, silent Shelah.

At the time of the funeral for Onan, the custom was that widows remained in the family home until the next son came of baby-making age. Judah broke custom, along with Tamar's heart. He sent her home to her family of origin with the promise, "When Shelah is old enough, he will marry you." So, she is summarily dismissed, rejected, and sent packing. The years pass. Shelah grows up, but he never comes a-calling. Tamar is to silently remain at her father's house. She is not eligible for remarriage because she theoretically belongs to Shelah. In disgrace, being a childless widow, she is out of sight and out of Judah's mind.

Oh, the pain revisited for so many sisters. Promises made and broken. Plans begun and never fulfilled. Hopes and dreams washed away due to the decisions of others, without regard to feelings of rejection and abandonment that won't simply leave and go away. Women without children were powerless and poverty stricken. Women without children and resources were looked down upon. There were snickers and whispers. Tamar spent long days and months and many years, waiting, watching, hoping, praying in futility. She stood at the crossroads, wondering what to do. Then she heard it through the grapevine!

Granny taught me that "every shut eye ain't asleep, and every good-bye ain't gone." So even though Tamar was out of Judah's mind, he wasn't out of hers. She was determined not to be the dissed, rejected woman. She was not going to remain the poor relation in her father's house. There had to be a way out. There had to be a better life. There had to be some options. So, she waited. She watched. She listened. She learned that Judah's days of mourning were over. He and his friend were going to shear sheep, and they had to pass by her father's place. Wisdom whispered a sweet something to her ears. Girlfriend got up, got dressed, and got gone!

Here is a woman who has experienced the most crushing of life's "not so good" experiences. She was married to a man who was not sensitive to her biological or cultural needs to become a mother. He dies. She becomes a grieving widow who, by tradition, has to dress in dark mourning clothes for the specified period of time. Then she's "handed over" to the next man. He takes from her and refuses to give her the seed she needs for pregnancy. He simply uses her without regard to the consequences. Death is the price he pays for that. She's widowed the second time. Then she's sent home. It's plain and simple rejection and abandonment. Finally, she's lied to and forgotten. Many of us are familiar with this story. Many of us think the game of life is over. Many of us give up and feel beaten. Tamar teaches us how to fight back. And she doesn't fight fair!

She becomes a woman who quietly awaits her turn. She is a woman with a keen and observant mind. She is a woman with a godly spirit who deeply longs to be fulfilled as a mother. So, she waits patiently for the Ferris wheel of life to move her on up. She is quite familiar with sitting on the bottom seat, which seems stuck. But she waits. She understands that God has not forgotten her. She comprehends fully that the wheel is not broken; it just requires sufficient time to move slowly but surely upward. As she waits, she keeps her ears open for direction to make her move. She is alert to the moments of pregnant possibilities that occur when we think all hope is gone. After years of waiting, her time has come.

It's wonderful when you know that it's your turn. It's a delicious feeling to realize that all is not lost, that God did not pass you by, and that there are some dividends prepared for those who simply sit and wait. For in her waiting time, death had come and claimed Judah's wife, Bathshua. In Tamar's waiting time, Judah had experienced the period of grieving and denying himself the companionship of female flesh. In her waiting time, Tamar had grown accustomed to being celibate. And she knew that a man did not have a woman's patience. She decided to take a journey of her own.

The woman who was thought to have less power and authority chooses to use the means available to her. The woman who has been played the fool by her father-in-law resorts to trickery and deception in order to fool him. The woman who has made an art of waiting dresses in the clothing of a prostitute and goes to the crossroads to sit and wait. Judah comes strolling along. She is simply a woman waiting. He assumes that she is a cultic temple prostitute because her face is covered, and she is dressed in bright clothes. He feels that he has been waiting for a long time. She knows how to wait. He propositions her. She hesitates, seeming to think of a price. But she's had the price in mind all along. She wants a son.

When Judah makes his request for sex, Tamar speaks: "What will you give to lie with me?" Feeling generous, he offers her a young kid from his many flocks. She responds, "I agree. However, I'd like a promissory note until the animal arrives." In her waiting she has become shrewd. She knows Judah as a liar and deceiver. She listens to Wisdom's voice. She asks for the three articles every man of worth carried in that region of the country. "Let me hold your seal and its cord, along with your staff," she demands These obvious items will prove his paternity if she's successfully impregnated. Just wanting to make a "quick hit and run," Judah hands her what she's requested.

Using the wisdom of the ages, Tamar has sex with her father-in-law. By using her initiative, she continues the bloodline of the tribe of Judah. She holds within her spirit that longing for a child. She contains within her womb the seed that allows Jesus the Christ to continue his journey through forty-two generations, because she becomes pregnant. She returns home, takes off the clothing of a prostitute, and resumes her posture of patiently waiting. The only problem is that you can't be a little bit pregnant. And a pregnancy has a way of becoming obvious to onlookers.

After sending the kid to "the temple prostitute" with his friend, who could not find her, Judah dismisses the promise he made: "Well, I tried." Life returns to normal for about three months. Then word comes to him: "Your daughter-in-law has played the harlot. She's pregnant." As the chief lawgiver, Judah rules that she should be brought from her father's home and burned to death. The old double standard is in full effect. But Tamar, who has learned to wait, sends the three articles to him in the meantime. Judah's injustice toward her rises up and slaps him in the face. "She is more righteous than I am," he sadly proclaims. He confesses that he has done the girl wrong. He has withheld Shelah from her. He has been an unjust judge. And the babies are his; there is no denial forthcoming. The girl is alright!

Good things do come to those who learn how to wait. For Lil' Sista had twins!

CAN WE TALK?

God will use the very thing you felt was stolen from you and turn it into your blessing! The secret is to wait your turn! God cannot forget that somebody "done ya wrong"! God will not leave you, dissed, abandoned, and rejected. God knows the score. God's got your back. And the good news is that God is on your side.

"Waiting your turn" may feel as if nothing is happening. Ever gotten into a checkout line that seemed endless? The clerk is slow. Everybody ahead of you has a full basket. You look for a shorter line. And when you get there, Lil' Sista puts up the "closed" sign! You find yourself back in the first line, with two additional people, with full baskets, of course, ahead of you!

The clerk is doing the very best she can with the customer at the counter! That particular individual needs her complete and undivided attention. And when it's your turn, she'll treat you in the same polite and efficient manner. It happens every time you "wait your turn"! Standing at the crossroads? Haven't received directions? Don't make your move too soon. "Wait your turn!"

BEAUTY AND THE BEAST: FOR THE BAD GIRL IN EACH OF US

Beauty and the Beast is a story of real true love.

For who can love an ugly thing? It's really unheard of.

But Beauty can be locked inside a very ugly thing.

It takes loving eyes to see beyond what lays dormant within.

I wanted to be Ms. Beauty—tried hard to be real cute.

I gave up my goods and let just anybody take my stuff.

My self-esteem fled the scene. Shame and disgust took its place.

I played a role, hid my hurt, wore a smiling mask on my face.

I knew that within I was the beast.

Myself I couldn't ignore. The things I hated, I had become.

Why pretend anymore?

But at the depth of my pain—when death seemed a sweet escape—

I yielded to love and was I ever surprised as

Beauty stared me in the face!

Mercy Saw Me!

}┥┥┝{

O NCE UPON A TIME, there was a woman of color who was discovered on a garbage dump! She was a wife. She was a mother. She had a home. She had a husband. But she ended up on a garbage dump. How did a nice girl, from a good home, raised correctly in a nuclear family, end up in a place like that, you ask? Well, it's a long story. And I can tell you that the road to the garbage dump is always a winding one; it's always filled with crooks and turns; and it's always the route of bad decisions, horrible choices, and multiple options that should not have been selected. The truth is that at one time or another many women of color have discovered themselves tossed upon a garbage dump!

So where do I begin? How do I explain? When did this distinctive journey originate? It's still hard to sort it out. But I can tell you up front, I never intended to end up on a garbage dump. I had plans, hopes, and dreams. I wanted the knight on a horse, the house with the picket fence, the little boy who looked just like my knight, and the adorable little girl who would be the spitting image of me. That's what Mama told me. That's what my world of women showed me. All of my sisters, aunts, cousins, and friends wanted, needed, and expected some man to make them whole. For one was never a whole number. I was well taught that you had to have a man to be complete.

Surely you know what I mean. Remember Sarah and Hagar shared Abraham. Hannah and Peninnah shared Elkanah. Leah and Rachel shared Jacob. Tamar had two husbands, but was forced to seduce her father-in-law. Naomi, prim and proper Jewish matriarch, directed Ruth to go and lay herself down as an offering at the feet of a sleeping Boaz. And that's the genesis of how David got here to rape and eventually marry Bathsheba. Sister, it's been a "man thing" since the beginning. This is no new thing. A woman will go to any lengths to feel complete. It's no recent discovery that the world doesn't like or appreciate a single, "making it on her own" woman. These women are talked about. They're labeled butch and b——. They're harassed: "Girl, when you gonna get married?" They're looked down on: "Chile, can't you find a man?" So, we will go to any lengths to be socially accepted. Honestly, I think my journey to the garbage dump began with my birth. For all of the social, cultural, and religious expectations said that I was inferior and needed a man to make me whole!

But I remembered Mother Eve, the Archetype of us all. I remembered that she had been created as a divine design. I remembered that she had beauty, build, and intellect. I remembered that she had been given the privilege of naming the world by God. She had the right to have dominion over her world. And she was gifted with the ability to make decisions. Oh, I know the bad press that Girlfriend has gotten. I understand the rap sheet that is out on Sista Eve. But look at her this way: she was an independent thinker. She was a skilled negotiator. And she was a leader. We owe a long overdue tribute to the sister!

You've got to give the girl her props. She was co-manager and equal partner in the largest corporation of the world—the Garden of Eden. She had free rein to superintend both property and creatures. God had told both Adam and Eve to "take dominion over the world and subdue it." That sister walked tall. She was fiercely independent until the Prince of the World came to negotiate with her: "Girl, you're going places. I like your style." Each one of us needs to be noticed, affirmed, and stroked. So,

Sister Corporate Executive stopped to listen: "Sister, you can do better than this. You can go farther than this. You can be just like God. All you need to do is eat from that tree God put off limits. Did God really say that you couldn't have it?" (Gen. 3:1).

Step number one to the garbage dump starts with your trying to rationalize, "Did God really say . . . ?" Honey, it's a set-up question. Girlfriend, it's a pull-down question. Baby Sister, it's a trick question. For the Word of God is so straight, so simple, and so understandable, the Bible says that even a fool can understand it. So, Sista Eve's downfall began with her trying to justify what God had said. Now God had told both her and Adam, "You may eat of all the trees in the garden, but that big, beautiful, stately tree in the middle is the one I've reserved just for me. You can have everything else in the world, but don't eat from that one" (Gen. 3:3).

The Jewish rabbi would always try to assist God's people with staying far away from violating God's law. Do you remember how we used to draw a line in the sand and dare folks to cross it only if they wanted to fight? Well, the rabbi tried to keep folks at least three steps behind the line. So he would draw a box around God's law to prevent folks from entangling themselves in a fight they couldn't win! In this confrontation with the king of evil, Sista Eve played the role of a Jewish rabbi. She said, "God said we were not to touch the tree" (Gen. 3:3). Girlfriend knew that if she didn't touch it, she wouldn't get close enough to gaze at it and have desire tempt her to take a bite of its fruit. Lil' Sista was not a dummy. Eve put a wide box around her limits to God's authority.

But the maker of garbage dumps played the girl: "Did God really say that?" Now, understand that with God, it's always a decisive "yes" or "no." It's a firm "do" or "don't." "Right" or "wrong." If you've got to twist it, turn it, struggle with it, and waste sleep over it, you need to leave it alone! But Sista Eve began to contemplate the question: "Did God really say we'd die? Does die mean physically? Does die mean spiritually? Does die mean spatially? Does eat mean bite? Does eat mean lick or chew? Does eat mean taste or swallow? Does eat mean digest it into my system? Did God really say . . . ?" As these questions swirled around in her mind, she was already headed for the garbage dump! The journey doesn't begin with your action. It begins with your logical, rationalizing, and justifying thought life.

Eve negotiated with the prince of principalities. You have to give it to the woman. In life, you don't get what you deserve; you get what you negotiate for. But wait a minute. Did you notice, Adam ain't said a word! Boyfriend lets her be the rabbi. He allows her to be the chief negotiator. He permits her to do all the talking. And he stands there, tall, dark, handsome, and silent. So Sista moves into using her power of choice. It's understood; there is no doubt—without question—we realize that she made the wrong choice. For she chose to disobey God. But she did stop, think, meditate, deliberate, and then decide to do the wrong thing while trying to move on up in the world. The Bible says that Adam simply reacted to her choice: "And the man who was with her took it and ate it" (Gen. 3:6).

You ought to get a clue, Girl. Just because there's a man in your life, it doesn't save you from a mess of trouble. Tina Turner helps us to understand, "What's love got to do with it?" Love made Adam accept the bite of fruit from Eve's hand. Had he not taken the fruit, he could have remained in God's good graces. If he had not received it from her, he and God would have been cool and tight. But when he took it and ate it, Adam did it out of sheer love.

Adam was the first image of the coming Christ. Adam and Eve were just representing! They represented you and me, separated from God—lost in sin, without a prayer, with a huge gulf between humankind and God. That separation had them hiding from God behind some dying fig leaves. Yet Jesus, the second Adam, stepped into our mess. Even before Eve and Adam took that first step toward the garbage dump, Jesus had told God, "Prepare me a body and I will go to step into the mess with them. I'll rescue them. I'll lift them up from that garbage dump." Love had everything to do with it! Oh, when nothing else could help, "God so loved the world."

Wait, wait, wait, I'm getting ahead of myself. That's a true story and it's lovely, but I was trying to tell you how I got on the garbage dump. For the reality is that I did go there. I did do that. And the question we were tossing around was, "How did a nice girl like me end up on the garbage dump?" Let me just be up front with you. My name is Gomer. You already know me as a whore. But there is more to me than you've ever heard.

Remember I told you that the first step toward the dump is your thought life. I thought I could do life in a different way. I thought I could plan my own life. I thought I could outsmart the system of male domination. I left home before the marriage makers could complete the arrangement of my life with my parents. I was fed up with watching my mother kowtow to my father and even to my young brothers. I got sick of hearing prayers three times a day that dissed me, put me down, and made me feel like nothing. Early in the morning, the shofar would sound, and every Jewish male would face the east. At midday, the shofar would blow, and the prayer mats would be unrolled. And every evening, the shofar would call, and all the males would fall on their faces toward the Temple and pray aloud, "God, I thank you that I'm not a Gentile. God, I thank you that I'm not a heathen. And, God, I thank you that I'm not a woman."

What's wrong with being a woman? What's the matter with my gender? What's the deal that I'm inferior simply because I was born female? That tune didn't play well with me. I decided early on that I'd never be like my mother and older sisters, just the servant of some unappreciative man. I ran away. I left home, determined to make it on my own. I thought I was going to do it my way!

I was young, uneducated, and without the protection of my parents. There was only one way for me to take care of myself. So, I became a businesswoman. I was an entrepreneur. You could say that I went into economic development, business planning, and advertising. I was my own best product, and I sold myself for top dollar!

Baby Sister, believe me, I wasn't a hooker. I wasn't a whore. I wasn't a call girl. For the men didn't call me. They came directly to me. I've had men praying. I've had men begging. I've had men down on their knees. I was a professional. I was a quick study. I was an artist and actress of the highest caliber. My reputation grew as my clientele increased. My notoriety spread by word of mouth. I didn't need a business plan. I never had to apply for a small business loan. I never had any business cards made. I had what men needed. I was good at what I did. And my name was spoken all over town. Gomer was all that!

Then God set me up with Hosea! Can you believe I'd beat the marriage arrangers only to have the Creator of the universe arrange my life with some preacher? It's true. I didn't go looking for Rev. Prophet. God sent Brother Boy searching for lil' ol' me!

Now let's be clear about the difference between a whore and a prostitute. A whore is one who gives her stuff away, free, without payment, and for no charge. A prostitute gets something tangible in exchange for her services. I was not a whore when Hosea came seeking me. I was truly an employed and working woman.

Hosea was alright. He was a nice man. But he had no spark. You know what I mean? Nothing sizzled. Nothing was ever passionate or steamy. He was kind. He was gentle. He was thoughtful. But that was not my idea of marriage. I'd had excitement. I'd experienced being called by my name, looked at directly, and appreciated. And now after a little temple ceremony, I was sent straight to Dullsville. What you don't know was that I tried to make it work. I gave it my best shot. I put up a decent front. I even resorted to lying: "Oh, it's so good." I tried trickery, deception, new nightgowns, new perfumes, new oyster recipes. And nothing worked. He was just a good man.

Surely somebody knows what I mean. If you ever had to get married because you got pregnant; or if you married someone your parents thought was a good catch; or if the fire has died in his eyes when he looks at you; or if you need hot, steamy sex and get a sweet, dry little good-night peck, you know where I'm coming from! I took it as long as I could. Then I started slipping out the back door while he went to temple out the front one. I wasn't going off to do wrong. I just wanted someone to notice me. I needed someone to say something sweet to me. I needed some passion and some fire in my life. So, I went back to doing what I knew how to do!

I got pregnant. I tried to act as if it was Hosea's child. But God told him to name my son Jezreel, or "punishment." Hosea was so nice about my whoredom. He took care of the baby. He never threw my mess into my face. He was so sweet. And of course I went back to seeking attention. Again, I got pregnant. This time my daughter was named Not Pitied. And when I weaned her, I got pregnant with a third child, and God had Hosea name him Not My People! I refused to stay in this sham of a marriage. So I left the children with him and went back to my former lovers.

It was a difficult period in my life. I had known a good home and a loving husband. I knew what it meant to hold my head up. But the people around me never forgot my past. The people around me kept throwing my sin up in my face. Even the men started to mock me and to make fun of a woman who couldn't keep it together. My clientele never picked up the way it had before my marriage. And I became a homeless woman, a bag woman, a dweller among the garbage dumps. I thought of my babies. I heard them crying in the night. I remembered their pulling upon my breast. I wanted to see them, to hold them, to see how they were growing. But shame and disgust kept me far away from Hosea and our home. He kept being a loving father to children he knew were not his own. And I ended up sliding down farther and farther into the garbage dump. I couldn't give my stuff away anymore! I wasn't even a good whore. I was just an old, former whore who was living on a garbage dump.

There was a time when I was really ashamed to tell folks about my past. But I've discovered a rare and often untold truth. Most of us never really decide to give our stuff away. We let others take our stuff! Ntozake Shange wrote a poem in the sixties about how somebody almost stole her stuff! And the operative word is "almost." For she woke up, in time. She came to herself before the rape of her self was complete. She made a conscious decision to prevent someone from stealing what she owned. Your stuff is a gift from God. You possess it. You're in charge of it! You have power over it! And too often you decide to give your stuff away! That makes you a whore!

There is this very painful reality that too many of us are whoring *even while we are in the church!* We give ourselves to whoever calls the loudest without regard for what we need for ourselves. We have little passion for the jobs we go to each day. We are not engaged in the sort of work that blesses us and others. We are miserable. But we go faithfully, giving our stuff away, collecting a few dollars, trying to make it appear legitimate. Too many of us are being pimped and hustled by the men we live with and the children we have brought into the world. At least the woman on the street corner is honest. She is not out there because sex is good. Most likely she's there due to both an economic need and very low self-esteem because somebody stole her stuff when she was a child.

We have been giving our stuff away for too long. In order to keep a decent place for our children, in order to have some male in the mean ghettoes and violent projects, and in order to be socially acceptable, many of us and our mothers have played the whore. When there is no love, no emotional investment returned, no thought for your mental, physical, emotional, and spiritual welfare, Girlfriend, in my book, you are a whore! Some of us are even whoring around playing favoritism with male pastors in order to parlay ourselves into some coveted position. Some of us are dating the pastors and the deacons. And you have the nerve to look down your nose when the rap stars call us "hoes"! Shame on you! Whenever you allow others to profit off your services while they confine you to a corner, Sista, you are a "ho"!

I've been there. Confined to a garbage dump. But one day Mercy came and found me! I will never forget that day. I had foraged around for a meal. I was so smelly, I couldn't stand myself. I was settling down to sleep away the night hours, praying that I wouldn't dream of my crying babies, when I heard someone calling my name. I tried to hide. I ducked and dodged. I didn't want anybody to see the shameful condition I was in. I wanted to be anonymous. But he found me, crouched down behind a big garbage container.

Against my will, Hosea picked me up and took me back home. Can you believe that he actually took me back? He carried me straight to our bedchambers and laid me down, covered me up, and called the household staff. They rushed to get me cleaned up. They bathed me with perfumed waters and rubbed my weary body with fine oils. They fixed my hair and made up my face.

The dressmaker came with the finest silks, with undergarments as smooth as a baby's skin. They called in the dentist to fix my mouth. They treated me with the utmost respect. And when they finished their ministry to me, candles were lit all around the bedchamber. I waited for Hosea, who came in quietly and just stood and looked at me. I looked for his disgust. I watched for his pity. I longed for his hate. But Hosea came and looked at me with merciful eyes. There was only love. I couldn't move.

He began to make love to me, standing there in the doorway. He had not touched me. But I knew love. He came and touched my hand. He looked me in my eyes. He kissed my eyes that had looked so longingly at other men. He stroked my face. He worshiped at my breast, which had suckled other men's children. He paid careful attention to my belly, which had housed other men's seed. But he never said a word. He started to rub my feet. The same feet that had walked away from him. He picked up the left one and put it softly against his face. He begin to wiggle my toes. I'll never forget the words that he said, "Gomer, this little piggy went to market. This little piggy stayed home . . ."

It sounds funny, but his care assured me that I was loved. His look affirmed that I was loved. His kiss accepted me. His whispering of my name lifted my spirits. His holding me tenderly in his arms let me know the love I'd been seeking all the time!

Do you get the message? Mercy found me. And Mercy is looking and waiting for you. My name is Gomer, but I represent the whore in you! The whole book of Hosea is a love story about how God continues to seek out the church from the many places that we've wandered. God keeps calling us back even when we bring all those little bastard organizations and clubs into the church and try to pass them off in the name of God. God loves whores. God is in the reclamation business and has a special affinity for those who will allow love to bring them back. God uses honest, reclaimed, former whores for use in the kindom!

Look at the genealogy of Jesus. There is Tamar, who seduced her father-in-law and was declared by Judah to be more righteous than he was. There is Rahab, a bold whore, who hid the men of Israel and made her way into the Hebrew hall of fame. There is Bathsheba, more regal in her silent suffering than any other queen we know.

And there is Ruth, a foreigner, and Mary, who was pregnant and unwed! And every Palm Sunday, the week before Christ's death, there is the anointed and anointing woman called Mary Magdalene, who had a horrible reputation. She was his friend and follower too. She poured out her love for him. She cried over him when the men didn't have a clue about his approaching death. Then she washed his feet with her tears and dried them with her hair. She did a reverse Hosea on Jesus. I know the girl played with his toes!

God is in the business of recycling! God takes "throwaway" people, cleans them up, and uses them in service. It was a group of old, reclaimed whores who kept the lineage of Jesus going. It was these old, reclaimed whores who made it possible for Jesus to keep coming through those forty-two generations. It's these old, reclaimed whores who are the real cornerstones of the Christian church. It was on an old garbage dump, called Golgotha, outside the city of Jerusalem, where Jesus allowed them to put nails in his hands and feet and stretch him on that old, rugged cross. He did all the things we know that are written in the Holy Book. But the thing we fail to mention is that after he cried out, "It is finished," he called my name and said, "Gomer, it's alright now. Girl, even you can come on home!"

CAN WE TALK?

Too often we search for love that is right in front of our faces! We confuse love with lust, excitement, and passion. We forget that sex is not really what makes the world go around. We forget that although love contains some excitement, some highs, and some thrills, it also contains communication, plenty of compromise, some lows, and some painful adjustments. Love is a combination of the best and the worst of our emotional swings. Love is doing. Love is being. Love is wanting. Love is taking. But most of all, love is a competition in giving!

Gomer, our model of ourselves, was trying to do it her way. And, Sister, this is an all-right attitude. However, we have to remember that we are created by God with a need for interdependence and community. You will never make it solely on your own. Even if you get to the place where you own and operate your own business, you are the boss, and nobody can tell you what to do, you still have a need for customers to buy your products. We need others to make us complete. When Sister Gomer decided to do it alone, she set herself up for failure.

In times of pain or loss of significant relationships we like to tell ourselves, "I don't need no man to be happy." And that's true. One is a whole number! However, we do have a need for male interaction in our lives. Even if you are single, happy, and independent, there is a need for a "safe and sane" male relationship in your life. We can't live with them, and we can't live without them, they say! But we don't have to sell ourselves to the highest bidder. Giving our stuff away is not what God is calling us to do either. Your "stuff" is yourself! "Stuff" is not simply another name for your vagina. Treasure your whole self. It is you!

"Stuff" is valuable. "Stuff" is essential. "Stuff" is necessary. And it is your "stuff." So learn to be more selective with whom you will share your "stuff." Place a high value on your "stuff." Don't sell yourself cheaply. And, for God's sake, don't allow anybody to steal your "stuff" without them equally contributing their "stuff" to you.

Standing at the crossroads? Hold onto your "stuff"!

DEBORAH — THE LIONESS QUEEN

It is my day. It's my parade. I am the warrior tall.
It wasn't my plan for my life, but I dared to answer the call.
Sitting under a palm tree, chilling in the shade,
I never thought to look back when Chief of the Army I was made!
He was a big and tall man, with looks and brawn galore,
who had the chance to lead. When he stepped back
I walked out front.
For I am the Lioness Queen!

Meet Judge Deborah!

⊢⊣⊢⊣

WOMEN ARE THE WEAKER SEX, they say. Women are squeamish, they say. Women can't kill a bug, they say. Women have no business in war, they say. Women ought to have babies and allow men to run the world, they say. Women are like fragile objects who need protection, they say. All of what they say may be true. But "they" ain't God! And God has a habit of using "weak, squeamish, baby-having women" to be agents of salvation and deliverance throughout the Christian canon. Two tough sisters, Deborah, an Israelite, and Jael, a foreigner, teamed up together and put G.I. Jane to shame!

Sister Deborah is a wife and a mother whom God uses as a mouthpiece. She has no difficulty telling the people of Israel "what thus says the Lord." And they have no difficulty listening to her wisdom and accepting her counsel. She doesn't go too far from the "home front." She sits in counsel under a palm tree at the crossroads. We are not given the reasons or the circumstances that call her forth as a judge of the Israelites. However, we know that judges arbitrated disputes and provided military guidance. And some people thought Colin Powell was the highest-ranking person of color in the military!

As Deborah enters the pages of biblical history, we find her in her normal and accustomed place, at the crossroads, under the palm tree. She has obviously sat there for a long period of time offering both godly counsel and motherly wisdom to all who seek her out. She has made this "her place"; after all, it's called the Palm Tree of Deborah. She didn't have a need for the ivory palace or butt-kissing attendants. She was a wife and a mother. She knew and responded to her primary responsibilities and then accepted the roles God chose for her. She was determined to "do it all and to do it all well." So as Sister sits, most likely snapping beans for supper, she receives a word from the Lord. She sends for the commander in chief of the army, Barak, and because of who she is and the reputation she has, Brother comes stepping. She gives him the message of victory from God. He cannot refute her words. She is a woman who happens to be a prophet. He does not argue with her. He simply replies, "If I go, you'll go with me" (Judg. 4:8).

Perhaps it was a wise retort. Perhaps it was plain sarcasm. Perhaps it was his honest fear speaking, because for twenty long, torturous years Israel had been the oppressed. For twenty long, hard, and difficult years, their army had not won a battle against the oppressor. For twenty long-suffering years, while the Canaanites increased their army's equipment and battle gear, Israel had quietly "tucked tail." Now, Deborah, woman, prophet, and judge, says that they will defeat their opponent. It's no wonder that Barak is taken aback! But Deborah rises to the challenge. "Let's go, Brother. Lead us into the battle."

Then Sister Warrior, with full confidence in God, goes on to provide Barak with further astonishing news: "Certainly, I will go with you, my brother. Just remember this. There will be no glory for you. God will get the glory for this victory by using the hands of a woman" (Judg. 4:9). And they said that women ought not go into battle? Without two wise and willing vessels, called women, Israel would have remained in that ancient state of brutal oppression. Girlfriend may have been weak, but she was also wise.

Israel finds itself in one of the continuing cycles of life. Since the very beginning, the people created and chosen by God will rebel, sin, wind up in a nasty situation, begin to cry out for God's help, and promise to do the right thing. God is found in this continuing cycle. God sees; God hears; God responds, after a time of punishment for sin, with deliverance and salvation. It is no new thing. This is no different pattern. It's the same cycle, repeated again and again. Israel needs help. The people have been punished for twenty years. God promises deliverance through Deborah.

We learn several things from listening to Sister Deborah. First, she teaches us that you can be used by God while you are doing what is required of you normally. She didn't walk off and leave her spouse. We don't find her acting out of character or trying to bring credit to herself in any way. She does not shortchange her previous roles of wife and mother. God found her where she was and used her as she went about her regular routine. God knows where we are. God is fully aware of what we are doing. God knows that our lives might not be glamorous, exciting, or overly stimulating. But if we put our minds to doing well whatever it is we are doing, God sees and notices our faithfulness. It's only when we can arrive at the grand conclusion that "whatever my hands find to do, I'll do it as unto the Lord" (Col. 3:23) that God can trust us with additional assignments.

Most of us are always preparing for "next": Where will I live next? Who will I date or marry next? Where will I work next? What will I eat next? What will I purchase next? Where will I attend church next? "Next" so consumes our energies that we leave "right here, right now" in a sad case of neglect! There's nothing wrong with planning. There's no condemnation in looking forward. There's no problem with envisioning or dreaming about tomorrow. But when you neglect where you are, you rob both yourself and God. Deborah stayed true to her "right here, right now" tasks of being Lappidoth's wife even while being used by God. She didn't get "da big head" and take off in pursuit of fame and fortune. God found her busily accomplishing goals in that very spot. And when it's your time, God knows where you live!

The second thing Sista teaches us is how to make the place that we are "home." She sat under that palm tree dispensing good news for so long that they named the place after her. It is funny how we feel that we have to chase down fortune. When my supervisor, who had surely been one of my chief supporters, was told that he was being moved, he came into my office and inquired, "Are you going to start looking for a new position?" He caught me on a good day! For it was the season of Lent, and I had taken a passage of scripture to hold onto for the season. It came from Deuteronomy 28:1–3: "If you fully obey the Lord your God and carefully follow all of God's commands, the Lord will set you high above all the nations on earth. All these blessings will come upon you and accompany you if you obey the Lord your God." I was not going anywhere, seeking anything, for any reason. I was staking my claim right where I was until God sent a blessing to run me down!

This truly has not always been my stance. Chuck is the first one to tell you about how I would always jump out of the boat in the middle of a stream! If something else looked better (the old grass-is-greener lie!), off I'd go, chasing it. Deborah teaches us the value of making ourselves at home until Blessing comes and knocks on the door. She sat under that palm tree and was comfortable. If I know the girl, she had all the comforts of home with her. She brought some food, some water for refreshment, and a project to work on while she sat in counsel. She had some mementos from home with her to set up an altar in this place where she dispensed wisdom from God. For wherever we are, it ought to look like us and remind us of whose we are at all times. People knew where to find Ms. Deborah. People could count on her being in her space. People came when she called. It wasn't a corner office in a skyscraper. It was under a palm tree where Sistagirl held court.

Finally, Deborah teaches us about being vulnerable risk takers in God's name. Older African American women used to say, "I said it. I meant it. I'll step back in it." When women said that, they meant that this is serious business. I'd bet my life on it. So, when Deborah heard from God, she was certain of the victory of deliverance. She had no fear for her life. For God had given her the divine promise of victory.

In God's time, Deborah leaves the palm tree court and becomes the Warrior Queen! She accompanies Barak into battle. There is no record of how they did the military strategy. We don't know whether Barak called the shots or deferred to her. However, we do know that she was right there with him, directing him to move full strength ahead as all nine hundred of the chariots that had distressed the Israelites were stuck in mud, and all the enemy soldiers were killed by the very folks they had oppressed for twenty long years. She had a firsthand, blow by blow, account. Nobody had to come back with a report. She was right there in the thick of it all (Judg. 4:16).

Now that's a good story as recorded by the Christian canon. We cannot deny that when Israel stood, stuck at a crossroads, it was a woman God used to provide direction, but the story doesn't end with the battle scene and a bloody field of dead soldiers. We move into another scene where another weak, defenseless, and powerless sister is at home, alone. Into her tent bursts the foreign army commander, Sisera, who has escaped the killing on the battlefield. Once again, the "little woman" is at home. She is in the place of women, tending the home front, while the brave men go off to war. And God sends the commander to her.

He comes running in, looking all wild and scared. When he sees her, a sense of relief comes over him. He regains control. He is running from mighty, empowered Israelite soldiers, but here's only a woman who knows her place. Sister Jael does play her part well. She is gracious: "Welcome, my lord" (Judg. 4:18). She is hospitable: "Come in; don't be afraid." He lies down and demands some water to drink. She is kind. She covers him with a rug and brings him a container of milk. He relaxes and gives her an order: "Stand at the door. If anyone comes asking if there is a man in here, say, 'No.'" Because he is "da man" and his authority is without question, he lies down and goes to sleep. Mother is standing at attention, but Sister Jael is not as acquiescent as she appears to the king. She is not as weak as he thinks she is. She is not afraid to kill bugs or men. While he lies there in innocent slumber, she finds a tent peg, takes a mallet, and drives the peg through his head (Judg. 4:21). Poor baby. He mistook her kindness as weakness.

In the meantime, here comes Barak looking for Sisera, leader of Canaan's army. Ms. Jael is awaiting Barak's arrival outside her tent. "Come in and let me show you something," she says.

He discovers that Deborah's word of victory, due to the intervention of a woman, is quite accurate. The formerly oppressed "kicked tail and took names" that day. And all of chapter 5 of the book of Judges is a song of praise to the mothers of Zion, Deborah and Jael. May each woman teach us to wait in place, for deliverance surely comes to find us where we are!

CAN WE TALK?

Waiting is difficult. Waiting can be nerve-racking. Waiting is not on our list of favorite things to do! We need to know that God is at work, even while we wait. Waiting is a school of instruction. Waiting is a university of education. Waiting is a course in universal knowledge. We need to open our eyes, intensify our hearing, and be on the alert for what God is trying to teach us in the Land of Wait.

There are blessings being prepared for us that are not ready right now. There are pregnant possibilities being prepared that we're not adequate to handle today. There are tests and challenges around the next bend that will severely undo us if we don't master the principles as we wait.

Waiting teaches us how to keenly listen for God's voice. Waiting provides supporters who can assist us at the proper time. Waiting shows us our resources at hand and helps us to assess what else we may need to do in this preparation period.

Waiting? Check out Sisters Deborah and Jael. Do while waiting whatever it is you're assigned to do now. Give your present role your very best. Pretend that God is your supervisor and payroll superintendent. Let's see how much better you can apply yourself. God knows you have unlimited potential. God is cognizant of your *inherent* greatness. God is fully aware of your destiny and the role you have been selected to play!

So do like Deborah. Sit down. Get comfortable. Be a willing worker. *Wait!*

LITTLE COLORED WALKING WOMAN

Little colored walking woman, where will you go?
Who is this person that you are loving so?
Will you risk your life, your future, and take such a chance?
Girlfriend, what do you mean? It's not for a man?

Follow Me!
I'll Show You the Way!

}⊢⟨}⊢⟨}

T HE YEAR WAS 1978. The place, Gary, Indiana. A young woman
gave her heart to the Lord and joined the church's Usher
Board. Sister Emily Coopwood, the pastor's sister, was the board's
president. It was a year for new uniforms. There was a light tan
dress for women, slightly cinched at the waist, cut full in the
hips, falling to midcalf. We were not allowed to wear loud, dangling, or noisy earrings. There were "acceptable" shades of lip
gloss, not lipstick! There were practical low-stacked-heel shoes
with no flash appeal. We were to be sharp, but not striking to
the eye.

To be an usher required training. Twice a month, on a Sunday afternoon, we met for the purpose of learning and practice.
There was a method to be remembered. There were signs and
symbols to be learned. There were drills to be executed for
smooth change of stations as well as for receiving and directing
traffic for the offerings. The Usher Board was an official ministry of First Church. There was a code of conduct to be followed. And there would always be proper decorum. No talking,
no laughing, and no gum.

Ushers were not to be noticed for ourselves. We were to be
an efficient team and a coordinated group of effective servants
in the house of God. Ushers were required to know proper con-

duct for our worshiping congregation. We had to have a grasp of local church protocol: when to allow entrance, how many could sit in a row, whether or not the center aisle or side aisles could be used and when. This was no slipshod operation. The ushers were the guards of God's sanctuary. We could let you have free access to find your own seat, but our practice was to ask you to "follow me." It was our usual practice to lead the congregant to a row, point out the available seat, and ensure that those already seated cooperated with our standard procedures and requests. We did our jobs with a smile, and we were deadly serious about our business.

When ushers do their job correctly, the entire church service flows more smoothly. Good ushers know their crowd. They know who sits where. They recognize significant people like preachers, choir members, and visitors. They know the best seats in the house. They know how to keep folks from walking all over you when they're trying to get to a seat in the middle of a row. They know how to point you to the necessary rooms. They know how to assist mothers with crying babies. They know how to deal with noisy teens. And they know how to communicate without making a sound.

Ushers practice. Ushers learn. Ushers know how to make their role seem effortless. They are experts in traffic control. It's no wonder that David said, "I'd rather be an usher in God's house as opposed to dwelling in the tents of the wicked" (Ps. 84:10). It's no surprise to me that Jesus came into ministry like an usher. He called out, "Follow me! I'll point you in the right direction. Follow me. I'll show you how to find a seat at God's banquet table. Just follow me. I'll lead you all the way from earth to glory. All you've got to do is follow me."

It requires discipline to follow the leader. It demands sacrifice to watch, heed, and imitate the one who's ahead. Naomi and Ruth show us two women who trade places as leaders. These two sisters detail for us the art of knowing when to step back and stay out of the limelight, and when to step up and call out "follow me."

The story begins with Naomi and her spouse, Elimelech, leaving Bethlehem, the "City of Bread," because there is a famine.

They journey to Moab and establish a home in the midst of "different" people. Naomi bears two sons, Mahlon and Chilion, who grow up to marry women who are Moabites. They all live in the same house. Naomi is the leader in the house. As the wife and mother, she is responsible for teaching her new daughters-in-law the proper procedures for taking care of Jewish men. She even leads them into a relationship with Yahweh. Then life takes a series of horrible turns.

First, Naomi's husband dies. Then, both of her sons die. Finally, a famine begins in Moab. Naomi, who has no male kinsmen among these Gentile people, can no longer provide for her household of three widowed women. She decides to return to Bethlehem, the city she left years before. She is bitter. She is discouraged. She is afraid. She is a woman without resources for survival. She changes her name to Mara, which means "bitter." A deep depression takes hold of this woman who knows how to lead. She instructs her daughters-in-law to return to their respective families so she might journey home to die. Her days of calling "follow me, I know the way" are over. There are no displaced homemaker programs in Moab or Jerusalem. There are no welfare programs, government subsidy grants, or workfare projects in place. This was before women's rights!

Both of the Moabite women, Orpah and Ruth, follow Naomi to the crossroads of Moab. They are crying, filled with fear and grief. They have no husbands. They have no sons. They, like Naomi, are left without resources for surviving as widowed, childless women. The three of them stand at the crossroads. They know where they have come from, but they don't know what lies ahead. Naomi feels they are following her in order to have her find another husband and have other sons for them to marry! To our contemporary ears this sounds far-fetched, yet this was the custom of the times. Naomi understands their plight and takes the lead by addressing it. She tells them, "Go home to your own people. I'm too old to have other sons. I'm just another empty, barren widow. There is no hope."

Orpah follows her instruction. She weeps and turns and walks off the stage of biblical history. She is not a leader. She has been a good and decent follower. She follows orders. So, she returns to what is familiar. Orpah is like many of us. When we feel that the resources are too few, the risks are too great, and the future is too unknown, we give up. Orpah walks herself out of a significant role in biblical history. When we approach life's crossroads, too many of us do the very same thing!

Ruth, on the other hand, takes charge of the situation at the crossroads: "Don't urge me to leave you or to stop following you. Where you go, I will go, and where you stay, I will stay. Your people will be my people and your God my God. Where you die, I will die, and there I will be buried. May the Lord deal with me ever so severely if anything but death separates you and me" (Ruth 1:16–17). With this covenant commitment, Ruth takes over the leadership role in the relationship. We hear these words most often in marriage ceremonies where couples vow to remain bonded in love until death. But these sacred words emerge from the lips of a younger woman for an older woman. With these words, a woman who has been following the orders of her beloved mother-in-law begins to sing "Lean on Me."

Covenant relationships are not about equality. Covenant relationships are not about "what's in it for me?" Covenant relationships are about a serious competition in serving and meeting the needs of another. These women were not "blood kin." These women were not of the same racial or ethnic group. These women, after the death of the males that had brought them together, really had nothing more in common except seeking survival in a harsh world. This was enough for Ruth. She recognized the fear in Naomi. She understood the depression that had taken root within her. She knew the common exhaustion of trying to make a living without a male as provider or protector, yet she stepped up and took charge. She was willing to take the lead to ensure that Naomi was not alone. At the crossroads, Ruth said, "Follow me! I'll find a way!"

"Where there's a will, there's a way," they say. Ruth didn't have a clue that God had used this strange and painful turn of events to make her an ancestor of Jesus Christ. There was not a thought in her mind that one day she would be in the genealogy of the One who will reign throughout eternity. She didn't know that love was waiting down the road and around the corner.

She could not have comprehended that her words would become part of covenant relationships around the world. But she did know determination. She did know that where there was a will to live, methods could be discovered for survival. She had ego strength enough for herself and for Naomi. Wisdom instructed her and encouraged her to prompt Naomi, "Come on, Girlfriend. Let's go make ourselves a home!"

In the '60s, the Staple Singers used to sing a song calling us to follow them to a special place—"I'll Take You There." How we sang and danced to this popular tune. Even though most of us were afraid to go around the corner by ourselves, we dared to want to lead others to this "sacred place, somewhere." We wanted to be ushers, without practicing or training. At the start of Jesus' ministry, he rounded up twelve disciples and began to train them as ushers into heaven. Quickly, they felt they could lead the way!

"Boys, there are some things I need to teach you. There are some signs, symbols, and signals of the reign of God that you need to learn. Just follow me. I'll make you fishers of souls and then you can show others the way," Jesus told them. For three and one-half years the boys practiced, learned, and got experience. They were just about to get it right. They thought they had the instructions down pretty well. They'd practiced traffic control and fed a group of more than five thousand, not counting women and children. They kept the crowd in line as the Master taught the course on the Beatitudes. They had learned proper foot-washing procedures and table manners as Jesus served them at the Last Supper.

They took their roles seriously. Peter knew his job was to protect the preacher. So when the servant of the high priest barged into the garden prayer service to arrest Jesus, Peter jumped into position and swung his sword. Of course the man ducked, and instead of beheading him, Peter cut off only his ear. Understand that the brother had violated "usher" Peter's primary principle: "Don't come past me. I point the way. And I didn't give you permission to see Jesus." Of course, we know that Jesus, the healer, replaced the missing ear, voluntarily went with the crowd, was tried, and then was killed on Calvary's cross.

He showed himself after the Resurrection, but the boys thought the "Usher Board" had been disbanded. Feeling hopeless, like Naomi, they felt their former roles were defunct. They felt like they'd been pink-slipped. So the newly appointed "head usher," Peter, said, "I'm going fishing." And Da Boys said, "We'll follow you."

Their usher uniforms got put away. Their three and one-half years of training were neatly folded and cast aside. With wounded hearts, dashed hopes, and grief-stricken spirits they went back to doing what they remembered. They were disenchanted. They were hurting. They were lost, without a chief. They felt abandoned. They didn't know what else to do. They went back to the familiar. They fished all night and caught nothing. They dangled the lines and bait, but nothing bit. They shook their nets—empty! They remained silent. They sat still. They waited. They watched. Nothing happened.

Of course, you and I don't know anything about sliding back into old haunts and habits. We're so good, so holy, so committed that we cannot comprehend being without hope or help. Being "good Christians," we're so faith-filled that we cannot understand running backward. But if you are honest and will admit to your own bouts with depression, disappointments, defeat, or wrestling with personal demons, you can identify with Naomi and Da Boys, who stood at the crossroads of their lives, stunned and empty.

If you've had to face failure or battle with your fears, you can relate. If you've ever made a huge mistake and your life has ended up in an overwhelming mess, you know this story. For when the going gets tough, the tough usually return to something that makes life "feel" normal. Mess with me, Life, and I'll go to the mall. Let life start acting crazy, and you will find me in a restaurant, in a take-out line, or at the corner market. Malls, meals, and my nail technician bring normalcy back to my life! When we're faced with a crisis, we want predictability.

Naomi says, "I'm going back home." The disciples say, "We're going back to fishing." I go shopping and eating. And the enemy of our souls knows your fall-back habits too. When crisis comes too often, we give up ushering. We start missing practice. We begin to slack off with church attendance. We make excuses. We begin to withdraw. But in the dawn of a brand-new morning, after fishing all night and catching nothing, Da Boys heard a voice inquiring, "Children, have you caught anything?" (John 21:5).

This is one of two times that we find Jesus calling the disciples "children." Not only is it a term of endearment; it's a call to them to remind them of their behavior. Wise folks grow to understand that if you continue to repeat old patterns, you reap the same old results. The disciples had not grown as much as they thought! In all that Naomi had tried to teach Orpah, she didn't get the message either! But Ruth caught ahold of a new vision of being. She saw the many possibilities if she stepped up and stepped out in faith. The Bible doesn't say it, but in my mind, I'm clear that as these two sisters, Ruth and Naomi, stood at the crossroads between Moab and Bethlehem, it was Ruth who lifted her foot first, struck out in the direction of the unknown, looked back over her shoulder at a shocked, still-standing older woman, and yelled, "Come on, Girlfriend, follow me!"

CAN WE TALK?

Leadership is not a position! It's an attitude. The songwriter says it best:

> I don't know about tomorrow.
> I just live from day to day.
> I don't worry about the future
> for its skies may turn to gray.
> So many things about tomorrow
> I don't seem to understand.
> But, I know who holds tomorrow.
> And, I know who holds my hand!
> —Ira F. Stanphill, 1914

RUMPELSTILTSKIN

Beautiful! Stunning! Elegant!
With a smile plastered over a bleeding heart.
Regal! Queenly! Awesome!
Crippled within by the tremendous throes of sadness.
She walked with dignity. Her steps were slow.
It didn't matter to her if she arrived anywhere.
She spoke with assurance. Every word was measured.
She was maintaining a secret, but very public lie.
Her days were too long. Memory and stilled voices plagued her.
The nights were too dreadful.
Who knew what or who would capture her again?
Life was not. Death would not. Healing could not.
The intensity of her pain never lessened.
The horror of days gone by tortured every moment.
Her losses were overwhelming. Her life was shattered forever.
Her body had been stolen.
Her husband had been murdered.
Her baby had been the sacrifice.
She was left.
Stunned. Silent. Sad.
Rumpelstiltskin had stomped his feet and played his best hand.
She would not spin straw into gold!
Nor would she simply disappear from the land.
She would survive!
Bathsheba was her name.

Dedicated to my humming/singing sisters, Cynthia Wilson-Felder and
Janette Chandler-Kotey

Bathsheba

ᛁᛞᛁᛞᛁ

Too many women have been raped. One cannot explain the consequences of rape and its continuing, everlasting, haunting pain. One cannot describe the humiliation, the anger, and the shame this act of violence brings. And when the rapist is the King-Priest-Warrior-Leader of your nation, there is no recourse in the public square.

David, the king of Israel, the man after God's own heart, the great slayer of animals and killer of giants, had summoned her with his guards. While she had been purifying herself after her monthly menstrual cycle, in the privacy of her own home's outdoor tub, the king had spied her as he stood on his balcony surveying all his land and "property." Lust had awakened within him. Desire was burning and was not controlled by thought or reason. He wanted her. He sent for her. He raped her. He sent her home. He forgot her.

She could not forget! The shame ate at her insides. The guilt plagued her mind. The sin ravaged her spirit. Yet she could not go to the Temple for absolution and forgiveness. Many times she tried to attend worship in the place of women. Step by step she moved purposefully toward the place of confession. She could not go inside. Around and around its perimeter she marched, a silent, invisible sentinel. She ached for community. She was desperately in need of care and consolation. She wanted to empty herself of the age-old question, "Why did this happen to me?" But she could not bear the stares of other women. Certainly, they would see her shame. She tasted it as a daily diet. Their pointing fingers and whispers of blame would only increase her humiliation. So she withdrew into herself.

"It did not happen," she thought. "It was only a dream," she consoled herself. "I'm imagining all this," she reasoned. Then her monthly cycle did not come. Morning queasiness came in its place. Tender breasts became her reality. She was pregnant. She was the tossed-aside whore of the king. There was no doubt whose seed was firmly implanted within her womb. Uriah, her husband, was off engaged in war.

She sent word to David of her situation. She waited for his wisdom. He plotted an intervention. He repeated his old habit. Guards were sent to bring Uriah home. His reasoning was to have this male soldier come home, engage in marital sex with his wife, and claim David's seed as his own! David felt this would solve the problem. Uriah could "father" his child. "No one will be the wiser," he thought. Bathsheba's "secret rape" was never considered. David's plan was to get himself off the hook!

Now Uriah was a man of integrity. He obeyed the king's order and reported home as commanded. After informing the king of the details of the war, he stationed himself to sleep outside the king's palace door. "No. No. Go home to your wife." Uriah replied, "No. No. Your majesty, our brothers are engaged in battle. I cannot enjoy myself while they are in danger of death." His valor signed his death warrant.

David was determined not to look bad in the eyes of his men. He wrote an order for Uriah to be placed in the front lines of battle where death snatched away his life. Uriah died a hero for Israel. David lived the lying life of a godly and upright king. He was, in actuality, a rapist and murderer. Bathsheba lived in shame, pain, and grief. She was a woman after God's own heart. The child she carried grew within her. She pondered their plight within her heart. Tears became her steady diet. Sadness covered her like a regal cloak. She had been raped, dissed, kicked to the curb, and widowed by the king of her people. She knew that Uriah's death was a plan to cover the sin of the king. She carried the burden of his lie within her womb. She needed Wisdom to survive and to maintain her sanity.

Standing at the crossroads of sanity and insanity, she could easily have succumbed to grief and pain. Let these ever-present companions bowl her over. Let wailing become her constant conversation. Let anger and depression consume her and take her to her bed. Lie there, comfortless. Blame David. Curse God. Wallow in pity. Cry, "Somebody certainly done me wrong!" But she didn't! She moved on for the tiny seed sprouting to life within her womb. She moved on, for she had a part to play in the demanding drama of unfolding life. She would come out of this situation. She knew this was not the end. I am clear that Woman Wisdom taught her to hum a simple song to keep from losing her mind.

Humming helps regulate your blood pressure. Humming establishes a calm center within when your whole wide world is spinning in chaos. Humming helps you to sort through the mess of your life, without losing all control. Humming is a gift to women from Wisdom. Humming helps you to encourage yourself in God! Humming is praise, without words, which draws God near to us. For "when praises go up, blessings come down!" Humming is prayer without words, which the Holy Spirit interprets. Paul declares in the book of Romans that we don't know how to pray as we ought! (See Romans 8:26.)

Bathsheba made it through the pregnancy. She survived a natural childbirth. She marveled at the tiny piece of love that God had created from such an ugly act of rape. A mother's attachment began the bonding process with the tiny, perfectly formed new creation. Then God "took" the baby as penalty for David's sin! Her firstborn child was born to die! Yet Bathsheba lived on, humming all the while. For when the words won't come and it feels that prayer won't work, you can hum. If you don't have a song to hum, you'd better ask God for one! It will carry you through.

David wrote the majority of the ancient hymns of the church. He wrote them out of his wide and varied range of emotions. He penned songs that have provided comfort to God's people down through the years. He wrote with passion and pathos. He articulated anger and adoration. He yearned and longed for inner wholeness and offered joyful praise when it was present. But where were the sorrowful laments of Bathsheba? Why have her whimpers of sadness, sighs of anguish, and the tuneless humming of her hurtful heart never been heard? We know that she was a woman after God's own heart. When you're placed in her situation, who else but God can you turn to for solace?

Every rape, incest, and abuse victim has a song. They sound like dirges. When your pain cannot be fully expressed through verbal articulation, you wail, and it's recorded in the heavens. Widows, divorced women, singles who feel hopeless in their waiting, each one left alone and unprotected sings songs in the long, sleepless watches of the night. When solitude is torture and even the stars refuse to shine, you weep melodies, and the angels catch their perfect pitch. Women who lose innocent children as a sacrifice to violence, those who miscarry, those who have felt that abortion was their only option, and those who ache for a pregnancy that never comes screech sounds of unbelievable range, and the Maestro of Music receives every flawless note. These are the songs we don't sing for the world. These are the songs we hum inwardly to maintain a sense of sanity when our world has gone completely mad.

Yet there is good news. We know the grand finale of this tale of sorrow and absent song. Bathsheba not only survives. She thrives. She makes it into the genealogy of Jesus as recorded in the first chapter of Matthew. Her name is not mentioned. She is referred to only as "the wife of Uriah." But what's new? We know how men will cover for each other and point the finger of blame at us. However, we have the inside scoop of who raped whom! We know she made it through every ugly circumstance that life threw her way. It wasn't fair. It wasn't pretty. It wasn't just. But we know she made it with reverent determination.

Today, Bathsheba is a type of Christ. For both she and Jesus were bruised, crushed, and afflicted on the road of suffering. Jesus was identified as the Only Begotten Son. Bathsheba was pointed out by David as "da one"! Because of sin, Jesus was captured, imprisoned, and held by Roman guards. Because of sin, Bathsheba was captured, imprisoned, and brought to David by his own guards. Jesus was sacrificed upon a cross. Bathsheba was sacrificed upon a bed. Jesus rose from the grave and the pain of death. He now sits at the right hand of God with power. Bathsheba rose from the grave of grief and depression. She points us to new ways of inner healing and has become a shero of our faith. Jesus died to birth new life into the world. Bathsheba lived to birth Jesus into the world!

This woman is a direct link to the Savior. She is a part of his forty-two generations. She didn't give up. She wouldn't quit. She refused to die in order that Jesus might live. She hurt so that he could live. She endured in order that he might become the Healer of broken hearts. She held her head up so he could be born to lift ours. She triumphed over her pain in order that he could be born to die and win the victory for you and me. She survived many mini-deaths just so that Jesus could win for us eternal life. Her name isn't mentioned in the genealogy. Yet she lived and she lives! The Bible says it's so. And if she accomplished what she did without a Savior, what in the world can we do with one?

If you can't see your way, if you can't pray your way out, if you can't confess it, touch and agree with enough folks to make it through, do like Sista Bathsheba, hum! Jesus had to have taken lessons from her. For as I read his seven last words, all the way from "Father, forgive them" to "It is finished," I can hear Jesus humming in between: "Father, I stretch my hands to you; no other help I know. If you withdraw yourself from me, then where can I go?"

We know Bathsheba's son King Solomon as the wisest man who ever lived. Guess where he drank from the fount of wisdom! It's very true that songs are missing from the hymn book of the church. The good news is that Bathsheba sang them all.

She has sung those howling anthems of women who live in silent pain. These songs are necessary for completion of the symphony performed for the only Healer of wounded hearts! I'm so thankful that God has given some women the ability to put words to our songs of pain. And when words fail, they teach us how to hum. Sisters, hum on!

CAN WE TALK?

Do you have a tune to hum?
　　Get one!

OLD MOTHER HUBBARD

Old Mother Hubbard lived in the projects;
she had too many children and not enough welfare check!
But she fed them all soundly and put them in water beds.
So she decided, quite profoundly, to run a day care for others
    instead!

The Persistent Woman

⊱⊰

YOU NEED TO MEET MY SISTER, Jacquie. She's a dynamic, powerful networker. She's employed by a federal corporation with responsibilities for finding jobs for skilled young adults. Jacquie is a walking resource center. Whenever we get together, she has a bag for me of articles, clippings, papers, Web site information, E-mail "stuff," and church bulletins to share. She believes in the art of direct communication.

You really do need to meet my sister, Jacquie. She's a living example of the persistent woman who had an encounter with an unjust judge in Luke 18. Not only is my sister persistent, but my sister is tenacious. My sister is relentless in her pursuit of her goals. She'll drive you up a wall. She'll make you go running in the opposite direction whenever you see her coming. She'll have you ducking and dodging if you try to evade either her insistence upon an answer to a question or the granting of her request.

You really do need to meet my sister, Jacquie. As a child she was quiet, shy, and withdrawn. She accepted her role as my little sister and basically followed house rules. She didn't give a bunch of lip; she wasn't always in your face; and she was never assertive. Jacquie was always considered a good girl. I don't ever remember her raising a fuss, arguing for her rights, or insisting upon having her way. She seemed to be on the road to becoming a passive, submissive woman.

But God knows, she's changed now! She's made a 180-degree turn and can literally be a tiger in your tank. Sistagirl won't give up easily. She'll write letters that are as detailed as legal documents. She'll gather supporting arguments and cogent examples to undergird her case. She writes copious memos, and she'll call and call and call again. She's not put off by answering machines, voice mails, or caustic human responses. She knows what she wants. She will design a strategy to achieve her outcomes. Then she pursues her goal.

Jacquie knows Jesus. Jacquie is familiar with the parable about the woman who knew how to plead her case and not lose heart as she sought justice from an unjust judge. Jacquie knows firsthand the practice of pushing, pulling, challenging systems, rules, regulations, and stubborn people. I declare, you really do need to meet my sister, Jacquie.

Women have been taught to be quiet, never assertive. "Men don't like pushy broads," we're told. Women have been taught to be submissive: "You're so fickle that it takes a man to make firm decisions for you." Women have been taught that we have to wait our turn to achieve equality and justice. "You're trying to move too fast. Just wait. Your turn will come," we're told. Women have been taught to be demure: "Never raise your voice. It sounds too strident." The woman in the parable didn't buy these teachings. Neither does Jacquie. If you want to have a quality life, be in charge of your movement through life, and get what you feel you deserve, you won't buy them either!

Jesus had been teaching about the in-breaking of the realm of God. People were speculating about how to discern when God would return to rapture the church. Jesus' response was that no one knew the day or the hour, despite the guessing and figuring that were going on. Then he moved into teaching about being persistent, faithful, and prayerful as we work toward the day of God's return. Jesus told the story of a woman who simply would not quit insisting that life should change for the better on her behalf.

The judge who has the power to grant a poor widow's request is labeled unjust. "In a certain town there was a judge who feared neither God nor people. And there was a widow in that town who kept coming to him with the plea, 'Grant me justice against my adversary'" (Luke 18:3). The words "a certain town" allow this to be anywhere in all the world. The judge has no name, which allows us the opportunity to put in any and every male power broker who has little regard for the poor, the insignificant, and the marginalized. The nameless widow is a woman without resources, without support, and with little hope for justice, as is the average woman in the world who does not have a male to mentor, advance, and uphold her and her children. At the United Nations Conference on Women held in Copenhagen, it was concluded that women do almost three-quarters of the work in the world on a daily basis. Women produce more than 45 percent of the food grown the world over. However, women receive only about 10 percent of the world's income and own about 1 percent of the world's property, much of which is actually "held" by men to receive "minority status" for "set-aside" programs.

> A billion human beings go to bed hungry every night of their lives in chronic undernourishment; the majority are women and children. An average of 50,000 people a day die from starvation and the effects of malnutrition: the majority are women and children. Even in rich countries, chronic malnutrition afflicts millions, mainly old people and families headed by unemployed women with dependent children. In the United States, 12 million children are without medical coverage and 5 million teeter on the edge of homelessness. Poor prenatal care . . . means that a baby born in the shadow of the White House is now more likely to die in the first year of life than a baby born in Costa Rica. (Marilyn French, *The War against Women* [New York: Summit Books, 1992], 38)

We need women with persistence to challenge the unjust power brokers who allow this abuse of women and children to continue, unchecked.

There are many nameless, faceless, voiceless women in the world today who need to meet my sister, Jacquie. These nameless, faceless, voiceless women are us. We need to band together. We need to market her persistence. We need to go and make demands of the unjust judges!

Capitalist governments and male-dominated labor unions colluded in keeping women in the lowest-paid, most marginal work. Everywhere, women were denied the right to work for decent pay on the grounds that men supported them. Since not all men did, women and their children were thrust into even deeper impoverishment, and men who did support women treated them like property—In the same vein, men-as-a-caste—elite and working class men—continue to seek ways to defeat feminism, by rescinding or gnawing away at its victories (legal abortions), confining women to lower employment levels . . . , or founding movements aimed at returning them to fully subordinate status (fundamentalism). . . . Men are adapting new technologies to old purposes. These actions amount to a global war against women. (French, *The War against Women*, 12–13)

Injustice toward women was prevalent in the days of Jesus. It has only changed slightly in our time! This parable is yet needed to be seen as viable and alive! We must learn, like my sister, Jacquie, how to be persistent in our pursuit for justice for ourselves and for our children.

The woman in the parable is not defined as young or old. We don't know whether she came from a family of means or not. Her racial background or ethnic group is not spelled out. All we are told is that she is a widow who was seeking justice from her adversary. We are not told the specifics of this antagonistic situation. There is no description of the opponent in this case. The lack of information given about the widow's opponent allows us to use our imaginations and apply our own variables to this parable where necessary. What we do know is that Girlfriend has made a serious decision that justice will be hers! Without a man to go to bat for her, without adult sons to intercede on her behalf, and without a political system that favored the marginal and oppressed, she worked the judge's reserve nerve! Jesus says, "For some time the judge refused to grant her justice." Like many male power brokers, he felt she was simply a nuisance: "Why bother with a worthless woman? Let my silence show her my contempt for her and her situation. How dare she come and seek to address me? Who does she think she is?" He tried to ignore her. He attempted to act as if she did not matter or even exist. He assumed that she would read his message of silence, get a clue, and slink away. Boy, was he ever surprised.

Early in the morning, she was there. As he tried to eat his lunch, she was there. When he took his coffee break, she was there. When he left his home, she was there. When he took his seat on the bench, she was there. When he tried to slip away, she was there. When he tried to hide, she was there. She began to show up in his thoughts. She began to work on him, even in her absence. He looked for her as he opened his cabinet to get his cereal. He looked for her in the mirror as he went to shave. He looked for her as he lifted the lid to use the toilet. For even when she was not physically there, she was there! She worked her way into his life. She worked her way into his mind. She worked her way into his dreams. She would not go away. She would not give up. She would not lose courage and quit. She wanted justice. She demanded justice. She pursued justice.

He was a male power broker who had no regard for God or for the people he had power over! He was insensitive and callous. He was tough minded and cold hearted. He didn't care about justice. He had no concern for the rights of women. He didn't consider her a person of worth or dignity. He had not had a course on the value of diversity. He had not encountered the issue of inclusivity. He knew absolutely nothing about affirmative action and human rights. Affirmative action and human rights were not cultural values that penetrated his thought life. It was not a sermon on the need to share power that changed his mind. It was not a coalition-building, networking caucus that brought pressure upon him. It was the tenacious persistence of one woman who broke him down! "Finally he said to himself, 'Even though I don't care about God or people, yet because this widow keeps bothering me, I will see that she gets justice'" (Luke 18:4–5). French asserts:

> Abandoned women are blamed for not being able to hold on to their husbands, for aging, being unattractive, or whatever faults. . . . But the problem is really systemic. Western society requires women to rear children in the isolated confines of the home . . . without pay, pension plan, or medical insurance of their own. . . . Even without external pressure, it is very difficult to earn enough to support a family and raise children at the same time. The system forces mothers into dependency on men. But neither fathers nor the state are forced to support the women who maintain society. Judges may award divorced women child support or alimony payments but . . . welfare is both demeaning and insufficient . . . this discounting of women's work—which is essentially taking care of all of society—has disastrous effects on women. It seems never to occur to men that taking care of themselves and raising their children should be everyone's work, not solely women's. (French, *The War against Women*, 38–39)

As we march toward the new millennium we need to learn some lessons from this widow who challenged the system and forced the judge to change his mind and act justly in her situation.

This nameless woman seemingly waged war all alone. She recognized that God was on her side! She understood that she was created by God, loved by God, and cared about by God. Jesus taught this parable to show us the value of never giving up on God. Jesus uses the persistence of a disadvantaged woman to illustrate how we are to pray, take courage, hold on, and work for the justice that is due us. I find it amazing that women, as a group, especially those of us who claim a personal relationship with Jesus Christ, have advanced so slowly and with such hesitation. This story is not new to the church! The key teaching that I find here is that God wants us to work relentlessly for the justice that belongs to us. God is on our side!

It is essential that you read all of French's book, *The War against Women*. She provides valuable information that will shore up our determination to pursue justice, whether we do it on an individual basis or with a group. French writes,

> In the twentieth century alone, the world has fought at least 207 wars that killed 78 million people. And, while states glorify the soldiers who fight the wars, most of those killed in them are women and children. In each minute that passes, thirty children die from want of food or inexpensive vaccines; in that same minute, the world's governments spend $1.3 million of the wealth produced by the public (between two-thirds and three-quarters of it by women) on military expenditures. This is the real war! (*The War against Women*, 37)

The new, yet old, call to family values and a re-subordination of women demands that we act in accordance with this, the Word of God. Of course, the political right-wing male power brokers are concerned and want us to return to our "place." Of course, the religious world and its male hierarchy got uptight, bent out of shape, and teetotally angry when a group of church women called a conference named Re-Imagining to order a few years ago in Minnesota! Of course, the Black Church has a cadre of males who continue to hold the power and treat women in worse ways than white folks treated slaves! I agree with Ms. French. We are involved in a war against women. But the cadre of men don't have the last word! We have a biblical mandate, a scriptural role model, and "a red letter Jesus saying" that call us to advance the charge for justice!

Sistas, it's past time for us to use persistence, tenacity, and prayerful determination to save ourselves and our children. Not only do you need to meet my sister, Jacquie. You need a personal consultation with her. Want her phone number?

CAN WE TALK?

Persistence is a virtue! Persistence is an art! Persistence is a craft that can be honed and finely tuned! Jesus gave us this parable. This is not just some little cute story from the Bible.

It's a role model for us to follow. It's a strategy for us to use. It's a method that works. It's a design that you need to practice. I really will not give out my sister's phone number! However, I know that you have some role models that God has already placed in your life. Watch them. Seek some time to visit with them. Imitate them until you can unearth your own unique method of being a persistent, winning, wise woman!

LITTLE HATTIE TALKER

Little Hattie Talker
got tired of sitting in a saucer!
Crying with big, red eyes,
contemplating her cellulite thighs.
For sitting only widens backsides,
does not assist you or help you rise
from places known as "Stuck"!
One day Sista Hattie rose.
Put her hands on her hips,
a song of determination on her lips,
Sista made a firm decision to
BUST A COUPLE OF MOVES!
Today, slimmer, trimmer, and more wise,
sometimes tears still fall from her eyes.
However, she shakes it to the east.
She then shakes it to the west.
Most important, she's learned to
shake it to Jesus,
who knows and values her tears,
and indeed, loves her best!
Strut, Sista Hattie! Strut!

Sacred Tears! Jeremiah and Weeping Women

┣╌┫┋┣╌┫

A T MY AGE, there are still many things I cannot do. I cannot play tennis. It's wonderful watching the two young African American bead-braided sisters, Venus and Serena Williams, winning professional competitions. But I cannot play tennis.

At my age, there are still many things I cannot do. I cannot swim. It's embarrassing to have a young grandson, Giraud, who loves the water living with you. On vacations and when he travels with me, the hotel pool seems to call his name. This year he watched me sitting poolside, with a swimsuit on, just dangling my feet in the water as he and his granddad swam. "Grand, let me teach you," he said. For I cannot swim.

At my age, there are many things I cannot do. I cannot tune. I'm a preacher-teacher in the African American tradition. I come from a line of singing preachers. However, when I called one of my sista-clergy, Janet Hopkins, and sang "Happy Birthday" into her answering machine, she called to say that she loves me despite my broken voice. I'm not a "whooper" because I cannot tune.

At my age, there are many things I cannot do. But I do have a specialty. Some folks would say I specialize in talking because I do it so much and with great passion. But talking is not my specialty.

Many folks think I specialize in writing since I seem to be perpetually working on some new book. I do see writing for the sisterhood as a gift of encouragement and an extension of my teaching-preaching ministry. However, writing is not my specialty.

Many folks think I specialize in being a good mother. I've raised three children, I've been involved in the lives of Chuck's four children, and now we are the legal guardians of Giraud. Giraud Chase Hollies is a much-loved grandchild. He is often in my thoughts, and his name slips easily off my tongue. But if the truth is told, I don't even like children! If birth control had been a viable, available option when I was younger, I would never have had any! But since I do have them, a woman's gotta do what a woman's gotta do. But kids are not my specialty.

My specialty is tears. I really do know how to cry. I cry easily. I cry freely. And I cry often. There have been many times when I have wished I wasn't such a crybaby. There was a time when I cried if I was upset or angry. But the older I get, the better I can cry! If I'm happy, I cry. If I'm surprised, I cry. When I feel the Holy Spirit moving in my heart, I cry. I tell you, with no hesitation, at my age I'm a champion crier!

Like the women of Jeremiah's day, I understand the worth of my tears. Like God's people of old, I realize the value of my tears. Like the ancestors of yesterday, I've come to grips with the fact that sometimes all you can do is cry. Crying is an honorable profession. When Jeremiah was prophet to Israel, women were employed as professional criers, weepers, and wailers. The Bible even records, "Jesus wept" (John 11:35).

There comes a time in the course of human events when tears are just plain necessary. Whether you are "together," "tough," or "bad," in periods of difficulty and pain you need to know how to cry. When you find yourself standing at the crossroads of disappointment and despair, it's no laughing matter. Then is the time for tears. When you arrive at the intersection of Sorrow's Boulevard and Suffering's Avenue, trying to figure out how to move, which direction to take, or how to choose which way you should go, sometimes all you can do is cry.

Jeremiah cried. As he looked at the conditions all around him, all he could do was cry. "The summer is past. The harvest is ended. And we are not saved" (Jer. 8:20). We need a World Crying Day. For there is no place in the universe where pain is not great. There is no city where violence and human loss are bearable. There is no area where destruction, decay, and urban devastation have not become a way of life. As we look at our cities, as we see the killing of our children, as we watch the continuing moral, social, cultural, and religious collapse of values all around us, like Jeremiah, we need to weep, wail, mourn, and cry! Jeremiah understood that his tears alone were not enough, so he followed God's instructions and called for the women!

> Consider now! Call for the wailing women to come; send for the most skillful of them. Let them come quickly and wail over us till our eyes overflow with tears and water streams from our eyelids. . . . Teach your daughters how to wail; teach one another a lament. Death has climbed in through our windows and has entered our fortified places; it has cut off the children from the streets, and the young from the public squares. (Jer. 9:17–18, 20–21)

Call for women who have a specialty with tears!

An African American man thought of the life of his mother. An African American man recalled the many seasons of her industry and toil. He reflected upon the long days of her laboring as a domestic employee. He considered her various duties in others' homes, only to return to their home and offer nurture, care, and guidance to her own family. He remembered how it seemed as if she worked hard, unceasingly—up with the sun, yet she was never really able to accumulate enough resources to retire to a "life of leisure." As visions of his mama's life flashed across the screen of his memory, he penned a poem in her honor that began, "Life for her ain't been no crystal stair."

She had faced multiple obstacles, formidable obstructions, and gigantic potholes along the way. Yet despite the twists and turns of life, his mama had made steady progress. She had moved forward. She had not had an easy time—this he affirmed. There had been painful days and tearful nights, but she had moved ahead, advancing, keeping a steady pace forward. She'd maintained her sanity, her sobriety, and her salvation. Mama had held onto God's unchanging hand. God had given her a mission. It was God who had blessed her with children. She was faithful to the ministry of motherhood. Her son remembered. He wrote with tears in his eyes.

The prophet Jeremiah looked at the people of God called Israel. He knew their mission was to be lights to the whole world, calling all nations to the one, true, and living God. Jeremiah recalled that their life had not been one of crystal stairs either. There had been enslavement, harsh toil, Red Seas, the wilderness of sin, giant-sized enemies, a strange land all around. Yet God had remained faithful to Israel.

Deliverance had come. Dry land had appeared in the middle of the body of great waters. Enemies had been destroyed, run out of their own homes. The Promised Land was a reality. There were fields they'd not needed to buy, plow, seed, or plant. There were houses prepared that they did not have to build. In all of the seasons of Israel's life, God had remained faithful. The people of Israel could not say the same thing of themselves!

Israel had a problem with being faithful. When times got difficult, Israel forgot God. When the going got rough, Israel failed to recall God's goodness in former days. When it seemed that dominant, ruling nations were going to destroy tiny Israel, it would cave in and be conquered by contemporary politics. Israel was in a perpetual cycle of forgetfulness, internal destruction, prayerful laments unto God, and divine intervention. It happened again and again.

The Israelites' mission ministry was tarnished. Their light to other nations was awfully dim. Their ability to remain faithful was in question. So when Jeremiah is conscripted by God to become pastor-prophet to Israel, it's with a heavy heart. For once again Israel was in a period of being overwhelmed by enemies. Severe destruction was everywhere. The Israelites were being challenged by seemingly insurmountable obstacles, and their witness was blemished again.

Jeremiah stands, looking at the people of God. He begins to script a symphony of pain for Israel. Tears fall on every page.

He wails in lament for the People of the Living God who were caught in continual cycles of self-destruction. He prays to a faithful God on behalf of a faithless people. I can hear the boy pray: "God, here we are again. The summer is past. Here we are again. The harvest is past. Here we are again. We are not saved. We have not learned that you are faithful even when we're unfaithful. We have not learned that you continue to make a way out of no way. You will open windows and take us through cracks when it seems as if we're hemmed in on every side. Yet here we are again. Stuck in the misery we've brought upon ourselves. Here we are again. Crying and lamenting instead of being who you have called us to be. Our mission ministry is not what it should be. Our outreach to those poorer than we are is insignificant as we wallow in our own self-pity. While turmoil is all around us, we're trying to cover up gaping social holes with Band-Aids and rituals. Yes, God, here we are again."

Jeremiah declares that Israel's wounds are great. He affirms that Israel's pain is real. Jeremiah agrees that Israel has great cause for genuine concern. Then he moves to break out of the cycle. He finds a method of coming out of the hole of depression. He designs a strategy to move the heart of God. Jeremiah begins to pray with his tears.

He prays, "Oh, that my head were a spring of water, my eyes a fountain of tears, so that I might weep day and night for my poor people" (9:1). God is not moved by our annual fall-planning calendars that too often start and stop. God is not impressed by our yearly goals and working budgets for strategies that have failed before. God is not even affected by our annual resolutions, networking sessions, women's conferences, and hoopla events. But the compassionate heart of God is moved when we pray! Tears are silent prayers. Tears are unspoken petitions for God to intervene. Tears are inaudible pleas to the only help we know. God understands and answers speechless tears. This is one of the reasons that I specialize in tears!

Prayer puts us in touch with the Master of Missions. Prayer gives us access to the Ancient of Days. Prayer connects us with the Comforter of Israel. Want to be God's woman? Want to be effective in your effort of being different this time? Become like

Jeremiah and his band of weeping and wailing women. Learn how to cry over the needs of others! For tears of compassion are prayers that God hears and understands.

Yes, I specialize in tears! But my tears are not of hopelessness. My tears are not of faithlessness. My tears are prayers to a right now God! My tears empty out emotions that crowd my spirit, mess with my mind, and keep me stuck in place, not hearing the call of God to move forward! My tears move me to act on behalf of those things I'm crying about. I can't just sit and cry. I have to cooperate with the Mover and Shaker of the universe. The world needs my tears. The nation needs my tears. The city needs my tears. Families need my tears. The church needs my tears. My tears say that I care. My tears say that my heart is moved with the compassion of Jesus Christ. My tears say that I'm willing to get up and do something to make a difference!

If all I do is hang my head and cry, then I'm in for many red eyes and stuffy noses. As I cry, it's essential to recall the pain and hurt that bring the tears while looking forward to see what work God is assigning me to do in order to assure a better tomorrow. An African proverb says it's a wise one who plants a tree that will never give her shade. We have many things over which we cry, but how many steps do we make toward correction?

You can cry over the conditions of our cities and urban areas, but will you pick up the litter around your house and that of an older neighbor? You can cry over the violence in our communities, but will you make a decision to stop yelling at the child who runs down the aisle at church on Sunday? You can cry over the plight of Africa, but what will you do to help the Africans, enslaved to drugs, alcohol, and abuse, who live right in your community? You can cry over the loss of young lives, but are you willing to work in an after-school program in order to make a difference? You can cry over the breakup of too many marriages, but will you work more diligently to be nice to the significant other you have? You can cry over being single, but will you minister to others in your same condition who are hurting too? You can cry over the plight of African American women, but will you honestly go to work on the needs of the African American woman who is you?

God collects our tears, but God expects us to work. God honors our tears, but God demands our wholehearted response to the situations in the world we can affect. Around the world there are problems. Pain will cause us to cry. Our tears can be those of self-pity that will keep us stuck in the same place. Or our tears can assist in cleansing our tired eyes, seeing a new vision, and then, with purpose and clarity, moving ahead to new life!

Sista Hattie Talker got up and busted her a couple of moves! She did some major reconstruction in her life. Her days of crying are not over, but her days of being stuck sitting and crying have come to a halt. Girlfriend is on the move toward a brand-new future. What about you?

CAN WE TALK?

Has Hattie taken a seat in your house? Have you been sitting in your little pity pot, whining and complaining? Then you had best learn that Hattie didn't stay put like Little Sally Walker! Hattie got determined to bust her a couple of moves.

Some choir sings a song entitled "Don't Wait 'Til the Battle Is Over, Shout Now!" This is what Sista Hattie informs us. When things don't look good, when the situation seems horrible, when you can't see your way, it is the time to get up and do something! We wait and we react to circumstances. Hattie teaches us that we need to make our plans and work our plans. Faith is about stepping out into the waters called the Red Sea. God didn't move until Moses put his feet in the water! Get a clue, Sista Hattie! Bust your way out of that pity party and move on up in God!

Lil' Ms. Muffet Gets a Shove!

Little Sista Busy Woman, whirling, twirling, hustling
with ovens burning, wanted Jesus to notice her. She had hurt feelings
and every emotion was churning. Into the room she burst, wanting
to give her lazy sister what for! Jesus, don't you see me?
   Don't you smell
my awesome food? Won't you agree that I'm the best cook in the hood?
Why, I'm president of the Pastor's Aides and all my much-touted
   specialties
I have made. But my sister's laziness is really affecting my attitude.
So I want you to make her come and give me some help with
   your meal.
You make her get up now, and come and assist me. Why, I'm doing the
work of three African American serving women. Good Lord,
   can't you see?
Little Ms. Muffet can't sit on that tuffet any longer.
I need help!

The Power of Our Pain

⊢◁⊢◁

S HE WAS CONCEIVED on the beach or in the woods, so she
was told. Perhaps the irony of it all was that her mother was
certain that it hadn't been in the back seat of a car! Now, knowing who her daddy is was a different story. "Don't know. Don't
care" was Mama's attitude.

For the first four years of her life she was bounced from place
to place. Nowhere was ever for long. Nothing was ever predictable, with the exception of unpredictability! Finally, her grandmother declared, "Enough already!" Her home became an assortment of relatives: a true family of chaos. Today it would be
termed "dysfunctional." Then it was called "home."

The security didn't last long. A fire in the house brought destruction, a death, and severe burns to her caregiver. A young
cousin ran to snatch her little body from the billowing smoke
and flames. Predictable insecurity was back.

A childless aunt and uncle, who lived in Chicago, came to
claim her as theirs. They were working folks who did the best
they could and made arrangements for her to be schooled and
sheltered. The aunt, a domestic worker, found others to tend to
her after school, and she became a latchkey kid. All in all, life
was pretty predictable. Chicago became home. Life was better
than ever before. However, restlessness, uncertainty, and unpre-

dictability were woven into her brain. Abandonment was an issue that would never go away. As a growing child she always sought methods and alternative routes to secure herself, "just in case." Whenever she was forced to go south to spend time with her mother and stepfather, her new parents had to provide assurance of the very day and hour when they would return. She had family and she knew security. She was desperate to keep it, at any cost!

Our foreparents taught us that school, education, and more knowledge were the keys to security. She believed. She worked diligently to achieve as much as possible. And she did! She earned a terminal degree. She became Dr. Insecure! Inside her, the uncertainty never went away. She refused to plan for the long range. She called this flexibility. It was fear of "it" being snatched away. She was never good enough. How could she be? Didn't both of her biological parents reject her, abandon her, leave her on her own? Even her grandmother had abandoned her! The burns had caused her death. She was certain that part of their giving up on her had to be her fault. She unconsciously reasoned, "I'll make myself worthy." She thought, "I'll become a helper—a caregiver—a necessary person to others who are in need." She did. It didn't work.

You can't compensate with outer stuff when it's the inner stuff that's missing. You can't simply determine to become who you are not. You can't cover up a gaping emotional hole with a beautiful exterior. You can't make yourself feel secure with other people and other things. She married. She had children. She was going to be the ideal wife and mother. Who did she learn these roles from? Was she imitating others, or making her role up as she went along? She'd gone to school. She'd earned the degrees. She'd gotten the man, the house, and the two cars. She'd had the children, a boy and a girl. She was the PTA mom. She stayed physically fit. She was determined to be "the total woman" while all the time she was dying inside.

She was a healer who couldn't even feel her own pain. She'd learned to mask it well. She was in complete denial. "It's just life. Everybody has to deal with some pain," she consoled herself. Life was falling apart around her. The happy home and family were not reality. She had all the right material things. She was powerful from a cultural viewpoint. She was "all that and a bag of chips." But she couldn't find her own personal power. She didn't really know who she was! Her tuffet was no longer comfortable. Life was demanding that she move. She found herself at the crossroads. What "predictable" thing could she rely on to supply security?

Like Martha, the older sister in the story of Jesus visiting with her family in Luke 10:38–42, she has the option to do what is dictated by society: "A woman named Martha opened her home to Jesus. She had a sister called Mary who sat at the Lord's feet listening to what he said. But Martha was distracted by all the preparations that had to be made. She came to Jesus and asked, 'Lord, don't you care that my sister has left me to do all the work by myself? Tell her to help me!'" With the exception of knowing their brother, Lazarus, we know little about this family's relationships. But what is obvious is that Martha is secure in her predictable woman's role of preparing, cooking, and serving. What she finds totally unsettling is the fact that her sister, Mary, dares to do something different.

Mary chooses to sit at the feet of Jesus and learn with "da boys." Mary chooses not to help out in the traditional cultural norms for the roles for women. Martha, instead of using her own personal power, goes to the source of power that she recognizes, Jesus, and attempts to triangle him into her scheme to get Mary back to a "woman's place": the kitchen. When a personal crisis arrives, it is our first line of defense to fall back on what is predictable. It is true that Martha needs help. It is true that to prepare and serve a meal for almost twenty guests involves too much work for one person. And it is true that she couldn't call a fast-food place for delivery service! Martha is in a pickle. She needs power. She feels powerless.

Ms. Mary doesn't say a word in this passage. She is quietly using her power of choice to learn at the feet of the Teacher. Mary has made a conscious decision to be in charge of her own destiny. She has affirmed her power of selection. She has taken ahold of an inner resource to do the different and daring. It's wonderful and surprising to note that there is no conversation recorded about the disciples feeling uncomfortable with a woman sitting in their midst. With their own cultural bias, it would have seemed natural for them to be on the side of Martha. Yet they remain silent in the face of Mary's inner power at work.

Power cannot be given to another. Power cannot be forced upon another. Power must rise from within. Power must be felt, known, and acted upon. Power is the ability to feel confident in uncomfortable places. It is the urge within that allows us to do more, see more, and act more in harmony with what we choose than the expectations of others. It is not uncommon to see women acting in the manner of Martha and going to the designated power broker, seeking assistance instead of being direct in stating their needs. Powerlessness is a learned response. Power is cultivated by the choices we make and the consequences we accept. Power doesn't always make you stand up and do something. Power is able to allow you to sit down and be who you have chosen to be! Power is about choosing to live up to your divine destiny. Power has nothing to do with material wealth and goods. Power has nothing to do with educational attainment, degrees, or social status. Power comes from knowing, depending upon, and acting in accord with Wisdom who comes from the ultimate source we call God.

Power comes when we learn how to sit down and center ourselves in God, accepting the divine plan and purpose for our lives. When we are centered, we can focus and see the path we are to take for our best good, which will impact the world. Too often we are like Martha, running, scurrying around, trying to accomplish tasks that will justify our worthiness to suck in this day's supply of air! It's then that we make ourselves the mules of the earth, attempt to carry all the responsibilities, and get so caught up in empty busyness that we forget to care for ourselves. Soon, like Martha, we are slamming pots, throwing pans, and in a tizzy trying to get some attention and affirmation for all the stuff we are doing. Running from task to task is a good way to prevent us from stopping to deal with the mess we have made of our lives. Doing is an accepted form of denial, allowing us to ignore the real attention that we need to give ourselves.

As Martha looks to Jesus to move Ms. Mary off her tuffet, she is surprised by his response. "Martha, Martha," the Lord answers, "you are worried, anxious, and upset about many things, but only one thing is needed. Mary has chosen what is best, and it will not be taken away from her" (vv. 41–42). Jesus helps Martha establish priorities. It is important that we "do," and it is equally important that we learn how to "be": "Be still and know that I am God!" (Ps. 46:10). Mary had decided to stop doing and sit to be refreshed and nourished. She called a time-out from serving others in order to serve her own soul! For only as her needs were being supplied in those dry areas of her soul could she dip down, bring up, and offer out to others. It is only through being immersed in the refreshing Living Words of Life that we have anything to serve to others. The world cannot be fed out of our emptiness!

It makes God no difference where we are born. Jesus was born in a stinky stable with animals and their droppings all around! It makes God no difference that we are bounced from place to place and that our families are unpredictable. Jesus' family "lost" him in Jerusalem and then thought he was insane! He made him another "family," and they weren't all that either! It makes God no difference that you don't have a degree or even a technical skill. Jesus never got a college degree and didn't go to the school of the rabbis. When he talked in the synagogue, the people were impressed, but that didn't stop them from killing him. Jesus operated out of his personal power, which came from and connected him always to God. This is a primary issue.

Mary is one of the most powerful women in Scripture. She is a woman of few words. She is a woman of action. She shows us that serving is not our first role in life. She helps us to understand that the total woman is not one who is submissive to the dictates of society and cultural norms. The total woman is one who has a right relationship with God and is comfortable in her own skin, choosing to operate out of her own personal power. She teaches us wisdom that is not easy to comprehend. For it really is difficult to hear, understand, and discern the awesomeness of powerful silence!

CAN WE TALK?

Do you know the circumstances surrounding your conception? What were the situations concerning your "family life" that wrote the script out of which you make decisions, even today? Those circumstances and situations don't have to continue to be your controlling force! To give us liberty, freedom, and liberation, Christ came to set us free. Stand fast in that liberty, and don't be bound and limited to what your crazy, unstable family chooses to do! We have this precious opportunity to be like Jesus and choose new family members whenever we find a need! Just remember that Jesus chose, as new family members, other human beings with their histories, their baggage, and their inherent disappointing behaviors. There are no perfect people! You don't have to pretend any longer. We all know you don't have it all together. No one does. Yet God will work through you just the same!

What is something that you've been wanting to try for a long time? Regardless of how dumb, silly, or foolish it may seem to you, plan to give it a try. There are many others who have wanted to do it; take a risk and make an attempt. In your life space there are people God has already given you to assist you with taking a walk on the wild side! Even if you fail, do it gloriously and publicly. You will learn a lot, and failing will teach you how to do it differently in your next approach! Go, Girl. The world needs to hear your unique tune.

Hey, Diddle, Diddle, This Kitten's Got a Fiddle

Hey, Diddle, Diddle, this kitten's got a fiddle.
What she needs to do is learn to contribute her own tune.
While stewing over yesterday, whining, and crying,
"I can't play," her wonderful instrument loses its unique opportunity!
For playing requires much practice. Sometimes
the notes won't sound real smooth.
But playing what you can will steady your nervous hands,
making those unsteady noises into notes which zoom!
It's all right, Diddle, Diddle, if you choose not to play
upon your fiddle. Other instruments are available to you.
The orchestra of life is open for every participant to choose
what's best for them to lend their unique sound.
There are high notes and low notes; wind instruments
and drummers too. If we all try to sound alike, our
harmony is doomed! Girl, there are no excuses!
Choose an instrument and play. The fiddle is not
the only instrument that life's melody needs today.
But, Sister, you must choose, practice, and eventually
even you will play.

Choosing to Play a Different Tune

⊢⋈⊢⋈⊣

W E WENT TO A WEDDING. It was the second marriage for the groom, but the first marriage for the bride. She is a businesswoman, a professional, and a leader in her field. At age thirty plus, she wanted everything to be just right. The candles were lit. The music was exquisite. The bridesmaids and groomsmen came down the aisles, while the groom, best man, and minister came from the side door. The pipe organ gave the signal, and the guests all stood for "Here Comes the Bride!" As she approached us, something was amiss. Her white suit was beautifully styled and very contemporary. She carried six long, fresh calla lilies, which were striking. A floral crown was attached to her head with a white veil. She looked complete. But something kept bothering me.

Finally, it clicked. The veil was already thrown back from her face. The glow, the radiance, and the anticipation of love were evident upon her smiling face. There was no mystery. There was no suspense. There was no guessing. We looked straight into the face of the bride. The groom clearly saw desire in her eyes. As he approached her, she looked him dead in the eyes. They stood smiling at each other as they declared their covenant of love.

After my initial surprise, I discovered I was quite pleased with her decision not to participate in an ancient custom that had demeaned and devalued women for centuries. A woman was not permitted to look a man in the eye. A woman's face always had to be distorted by a veil. Only after the dowry had been paid and she became the official property of a man could she be unveiled. This woman was having none of that. She threw the veil off her own face and came down the aisle with boldness. She played a different tune!

A veil will not allow the real and authentic individual to be seen. When Moses went to spend time with God upon Mount Sinai, he was in the presence of the God of Hosts, and that reflected glory caused Moses' face to shine with God's image. The people could not stand to see the glory. Moses' shining face, with its mirror image, caused each one of them to realize just how far they were from God! It's necessary to remember that this was the second time that Moses had received God's laws. The first time, before Moses had returned, the people had forgotten God's standards, God's intentions, and God's plans for them to be light, salt, and examples to a lost world. But God's glory is easily and quickly forgotten by us. It happens all the time!

A miracle happens in our lives, healing occurs, forgiveness is granted, a relationship is restored, and we know we have been recipients of God's awesome radiance. We have seen God's glory. However, with the passing of days, with the changes of life, and with our human fickleness, God's glory fades, and the veil of forgetfulness covers our hearts. Paul talks about how the veil in 2 Corinthians 3:7–18 was a distorted illusion that Moses wore to cover up the fading glory of God. This kept the people from seeing that the longer Moses stayed away from God, the less brilliant, the less radiant he became. This is a different view of the veil. This is just the opposite of wearing the veil to keep the glory from scaring people. This was an optical illusion to fool people into thinking that God's presence was still as awesome and as powerful as before. Time and distance away from God's presence will cause all glory to fail. Yours and mine!

Sometimes we wear veils to cover our fading glory. When we wish to be less than honest about our intentions, we veil our answers, trying to cover up the truth. When we get angry or

hurt, we veil our wounded egos with threats or unreal promises. We talk in riddles, won't communicate clearly or answer
directly because we want to cover up and control situations.
Often our veils take on a life of their own. We decorate our
veils, embellish them, for example, when we begin to justify our
favorite prejudice, bias, favorite sin, and unpopular opinion.
Oftentimes we want to know the intentions of others without
revealing where we stand on an issue. We know that we are
called to work for peace and justice, but we will hide behind
the veil of law and order. God demands that we forgive, but
behind our veils we simply tolerate. The role of a Christlike one
is to be loving, giving, and caring. However, with a veil in place,
we can offer pity and give money! The good news is that we can
choose not to play this tune.

Veils hide our reluctance to change. Veils cover our unchanged
hearts. Veils distort our image with deception, lies, and hypoc-
risy. And veils make us forget who we really are. We can hide
behind veils for so long that we seriously can't remember who
the real us used to be! But thank God for Jesus who comes to
unveil truth. Jesus changes our hearts and our minds. Jesus
helps us discard the veils that distort our vision and cloud our
minds. Jesus helps us see the worth of every individual and
helps us value the person that was created from before "The
Beginning." Jesus Christ comes to cast light upon every ob-
scure corner of our lives and invites us to throw back our veils,
be open, be vulnerable, and be honest with the world!

The metaphor of Moses and the veil has stuck in our minds
because it was unusual for a man to wear a veil. Women always
had to wear veils to keep their sexuality, desirability, or ugliness
from being obvious. Remember that Jacob worked an additional
seven years to wed Rachel, whom he loved, because he was
tricked into marrying Leah, who wore a veil on their wedding
day! She was not as attractive as Rachel, but the veil and down-
cast eyes helped her father, Laban, to deceive Jacob. It was only
in the privacy of her own home that a woman could be unveiled. What must Leah have felt as Jacob lifted up that veil?

This unveiling calls us to be like the bodacious bride and
walk with our faces uncovered. We are free from this custom.

We can come directly into the "Sonlight" and allow our hearts to be transformed, worthy of being unveiled. For being in Christ's presence changes us, liberates us, and reminds us of just how loved we are. The veil in Jerusalem's Temple, which kept us separated from God, was split on the day of crucifixion. No longer do we have to look at another's fading glory and be deceived. Jesus has given us full access to the brightness, the awesomeness, and the glory of God. Look full into God's wonderful face, and let that glory be reflected through your life.

Like that beautiful bride did, tell the world to look a little closer, I've been changed. My life has been rearranged. I've been in God's presence and been made brand-new. Just look a little closer. God will do it for you! She came down the aisle with an open, unveiled face. A look of love was obviously upon her face. She did not turn to look at us. Her eyes were focused, fixed on the object of her love. She had made a decision to wed the man of her dreams. She walked in confidence and wanted him, and everyone, to see the look of love upon her unveiled face.

Jesus comes to us unveiled. The Suffering Savior offers himself to us as broken pieces of bread and crushed grapes made wine. His love for us is undisguised. Ours for him and for each other can be the same! The world is filled with so many options of colors, sizes, shapes, opinions—choices too numerous to name. But we can learn through the voice of Wisdom how to be so authentic that we do not choose to have others dictate our lives. And we will not be thrown into confusion and chaos when others who dictate come at us with the unfamiliar or with disapproval. Girlfriend initiated an action that was unconventional and had been untried in my limited world experience. But she was so self-confident because Wisdom had buoyed her decision to be different! And she was!

CAN WE TALK?

There are more ice cream choices than simply vanilla or chocolate. There are more choices for our clothes than just black or white. There are more options available than "to be or not to be." We can make decisions. We don't have to be like "the crowd."

We can move to a place of difference! We can even be like the bride and make a bold move! Take off your "veils" and let the world see the glory of God in the authentic you. We can wear "veils" for only so long until we "forget" who we really are.

I recall my early days of trying to "unveil." I bought a "mask" pin and wore it on every occasion! People thought it was a nice piece of jewelry. I knew it was my visible symbol to take off my many veils. I came to know, love, and appreciate the Linda I discerned beneath my veils!

They yet sell "mask" pins! Get you one!

BAA, BAA, BLACK SHEEP!

Baa, Baa, Black Sheep, have you any wool?
Bet your sweet bippy. I've got many bags full!
Am I not a little sheep? Although my coat is black,
there are many tricks up my short sleeves to
prevent me and mine from suffering lack.
I can do the hustle and the bustle.
I learned to slip and to glide.
For long ago I realized that a little black sheep
had to discover different methods in order to survive.
I could not depend on "pretty."
I was "the other" in this mighty herd of white.
While they thought black meant dumb—
I had endurance in my sight.
I learned to be real quiet, kept my nose to the grind.
While others were depending on playing cute
I had survival and destiny always in mind.
I'm set for life! My children's future is secure!
I may be a dumb-looking black sheep, but
my bank accounts, stock investments, and diverse holdings
are guaranteed to endure. And you know what?
More black sheep are coming behind me!
It's a big strong line of black sheep. And they
won't be crying, "Baa, Baa!"

When the Prize Patrol
Doesn't Show Up!

|>|<|>|<|

THE DAY HAD ALMOST ENDED, and Mista Chuck was still dressed in "church" clothes. He had removed his sport coat, but had put a nice sweater on to cover his shirt and tie. Knowing my husband like I do, I found his behavior quite unusual since his normal choice of garb is work clothes. He's a tinkerer, a fiddler, and a "gotta do something" type. But I didn't question his clothing. I went and prepared for bed. Just before the ten o'clock news came on, he stuck his head in the bedroom door. "Honey, do you think it's too late for them to come by?" he inquired. "Who are you expecting?" I asked. "Why, the prize patrol. I was sure that they had picked us. I got a letter saying I was almost guaranteed to be the winner." Did I laugh? Of course not. I like this man I married almost thirty years ago. I simply agreed with him that it was likely that the prize patrol was not stopping at our house on this particular Super Bowl Sunday!

The next morning, I called my sista-clergy friend, Janet Hopkins, to give her a laugh about Chuck's seriousness in waiting. She replied, "Girl, I had to run over to the church for a meeting. I left a note on the door of the parsonage: 'Dear Dick and Ed, I'm across the lot at the church. Come over there!'"

So, I guess there are lots of people who are waiting for the prize patrol to show up! Chuck is not alone. The question comes to me as I think of those folks waiting: What do they do in the meantime? Is their waiting a passive stance or one where they have a plan to fall back on when the van does not roll up to the door? Chuck is retired and has been for almost twenty years. Yet he works a steady nine-to-five job to supplement our income. His waiting is active. And so is mine.

I'd like to wait on the patrol. I have plenty of dreams and hopes about what I'd do if they showed up. I found a huge cathedral-ceilinged mansion in the Grand Bahamas with a gated yard and red lions on each of its four pillars. I can see myself there, writing, entertaining, and living large. I would put money into three checking accounts for my always needy adult kids and send them letters that for the next year "Mother is unavailable!" Then Chuck, Giraurd, and I would charter a small jet and fly off on a year of grand peace, serenity, and glorious mall shopping. But until then, I work nine to five, come home and work five to twelve, and when I'm back loaded with writing assignments, put in overtime. For if the prize patrol never shows up, I plan to keep living!

Women looking for economic security is no new issue. If we look closely at the lives of women, most of their decisions stem from their questions about money. I am persuaded that the Monica Lewinsky affair was all about money and financial security. Many folks have spent long hours, lost much sleep, and had their names much maligned due to this woman's search for political advancement and independence. There is some old, wealthy man who has already paid Paula Jones for her public trashing of Bill Clinton. There is a group of men who have helped fix her nose, clean up her act, and make her look more credible to America and its media-hounds. For if the public accepts her, they will have a tendency to reject the president.

Neither of these women has great intellectual capacity. Neither one is a great beauty, making heads turn whenever she enters a room. Neither one was born with a silver spoon in her mouth, which helped both of them appear to be victims rather than money-hungry attention-getters. Each woman allowed her body to be used to entrap a man whose weakness for sex is well known. Truly, Bill Clinton is not innocent, and neither are they.

Neither Monica, Paula, nor Anita Hill, our own internal scandal initiator, had a powerful man in her life. Not one of them had strong support from a visible male to act on her behalf. It's fairly obvious that not one of them was seriously involved with a "free" man who could stand by her side, give credibility to her "innocence," or offer comfort when the media and the public dumped her like yesterday's trash. Their tales are not new. It's an old, old story of women seeking avenues for survival when the prize patrol doesn't show up.

The story of Samson and Delilah is well known. We have been told that Delilah, like Eve, was a woman responsible for a "good man's" downfall. The finger of blame has always been pointed at Delilah. But a careful reading of this biblical story provides another view of the details. I can guarantee that if the Philistines have a recorded history anywhere, Delilah is one of their heroines. The woman was bold. The sister was direct. The sister was all that and a bag of chips! As the young folks say, "She had it going on." And a group of powerful men asked her to assist entrapping a man who had a weakness for sex! They offered her much money. Girlfriend was going to be set for life. Who could pass up a deal like that?

Samson was born to a good man and his barren wife. The angel of God appeared to the unnamed woman and told her, "You will conceive and give birth to a son. No razor may be used on his head because the boy is to be a Nazirite, set apart to God from birth, and he will begin the deliverance of Israel from the hands of the Philistines" (Judg. 13:1–5). As with most men, her spouse could not receive this "word from the Lord" through the mouth of a woman, so God sent the angel back while they were both in the same place. Samson was born, and it was known that "the Spirit of the Lord was stirring him" (13:25). But Samson was one sandwich short of a full picnic, and his parents gave him too much latitude.

Chapter 14 reveals Samson's fancy for foreign women. He falls in love with a young Philistine woman. Don't forget—the reason for Samson's birth is to assist in delivering the people of Israel from the oppression of the Philistines. His parents try to intervene, but Samson, the hardhead, is stubborn and marries her. Because he is strong willed and quick tempered, the marriage is never consummated: "Burning with anger, he went up to his father's house. And Samson's wife was given to the friend who had attended him at his wedding" (14:19–20). When his anger simmers down and he goes back to reclaim his wife, he discovers that his father-in-law has given his wife away (15:1–3)! Samson takes his anger out on the whole Philistine community and then spends the next twenty years leading Israel (15:20).

We want to believe that all of the judges were righteous, upstanding, and morally clean. That's how we like to think of our elected public officials. However, our thinking a situation is nice or ideal does not make it so. It's recorded that Samson had a penchant for prostitutes (16:1–3). Then "some time later, he fell in love with a woman from the valley of Sorek, whose name was Delilah" (16:4). The five Philistine rulers from the areas of Ashdod, Ashkelon, Ekron, Gath, and Gaza came together in order to stop Samson's deliverance from their oppression. They knew his weakness for Philistine women. It was his downfall. The "brotherhood" conspired together and went to pay a visit to Ms. Delilah.

There is no mention of Delilah's father, brother, or male relatives. There is no male to be her go-between. The five rulers come to deal with her directly: "See if you can lure Samson into showing you where the secret of his great strength lies. . . . Each one of us will give you eleven hundred shekels of silver" (16:5). Read it for yourself. Eleven hundred pieces of silver times five equals an awful lot of money in anyone's eyes. And for a woman with no visible family support or significant man in her life, who else was going to be responsible for her livelihood? She would be set for life. She would be independently wealthy. She would be able to live "the good life." All she had to do was to discover the source of Samson's strength. It was not an illegal deal. It was not a covert assignment that required deceit and manipulation. It was not some sordid sexual game of entrapment. We never read that she fell in love with him. Samson fell in love with her, and he has shown us his habit of choosing women who are wrong for him. Delilah was innocent of guile. She was simply a woman who did what a woman had to do!

She is direct: "Samson, tell me the secret of your great strength and how you can be tied up and subdued" (16:6). This is her opening conversation with him: "Samson, you made a fool of me; you lied to me. Come on, tell me how you can be tied" (v. 10). Is this direct or not? Another time she says, "You have been making a fool of me and lying to me. Tell me how you can be tied" (v. 13). Finally, she questions, "How can you say you love me when you won't confide in me? This is the third time you have made a fool of me" (v. 15). Then the Bible commentator goes on to supply: "With such nagging she prodded him day after day till he was tired to death. So, he told her everything. . . . Having put him to sleep on her lap, she called a man to shave off the seven braids of his hair, and so began to subdue him. And his strength left him. . . . But he did not know that the Lord had left him" (vv. 16–20).

It is odd how the blame has always been put on Delilah when it's fairly obvious to me that Samson's personal choices brought him down. He was a foolish man. He was a led by his sexual needs and not by the Spirit of God. He was always in the wrong place, with the wrong people, doing the wrong thing. His anger got in his way. And he talked too much to foreigners about his assignment from God. He got just what he went after. Delilah was the woman he chose to love. She made him feel good. She babied him, coaxed him, cuddled him, and made him feel comfortable enough to fall asleep in her lap. Then he opened wide his mouth and told her the secret himself. She asked him. He answered her. He trusted her. She did not dupe him or betray him. She kept trying to find out his secret, and he let down his guard. Delilah used what she had to get what she wanted. She was determined to survive and thrive, financially secure. And let's not forget, the brotherhood of rulers came looking for her. She didn't go out looking for ways to destroy Samson.

Men don't want to hear this type of exegesis. Men don't want to admit that there are many powerful brothers who are led by their *other* head! Men don't want us to know that many of them are out there, with their big, bad, bold selves, looking to lay their heads in "mama's" lap. Men don't want it known that in the nighttime, when it's the right time to be with the one you love, many a loose lip has sunk many a tight ship! Samson and the men who uphold him are pitiful excuses. My study Bible gives a horrible picture of Delilah, calling her cold, calculating, with honey on her lips and poison in her heart. It goes so far as to say that Delilah took advantage of him! The story demonizes a woman who was determined to survive.

It's serious business to look out for tomorrow. It's still a man's world, and women have smaller retirement portfolios and less earned credits for living beyond their work years. It bears repeating that if there are Philistine annals, Delilah is recorded as a shrewd woman who helped defeat the powerful Israelite judge: "The rulers of the Philistines assembled to offer a great sacrifice to Dagon, their god, and to celebrate, saying, 'Our god has delivered Samson, our enemy into our hands'" (16:23). They got their money's worth from a serious working woman. I applaud the woman's candor, honesty, and forthrightness of approach. To me, these are her redeeming qualities. It certainly wasn't her fault that he couldn't keep his mouth shut!

CAN WE TALK?

What is the condition of your retirement account? I pray you are not waiting on the prize patrol van. And I hope you are not depending on social security and Medicare to take care of you in your old age. It is imperative that women secure their financial futures! This is not an option. And it is something that even a domestic employee, child-care provider, or waitress needs to be serious about. It does not take great capital to begin an investment account. You don't need a degree in finances or economics. There are free seminars on investing offered in every daily paper. Women are getting together, forming investment clubs, pooling both knowledge and money to get caught up on the money game. It's true that we started behind the rest of the pack. But unless you are Monica, Paula, Anita, or Delilah, most likely the town rulers won't be stopping by your house to make a sweet deal with you! So it's time to get busy and find your own nest egg and make it work for you! You'll sleep better at night, and at age seventy you won't be singing, "Baa, Baa!"

Rapunzel, Rapunzel, Let Down Your Hair; or, Girlfriend, Take Out Your Weave!

Rapunzel, Rapunzel, Sister, please let down your hair.
There is a whole wide hurting world in need of your care.
Girlfriend, it's all right if your hair is paid for or even borrowed.
Just let it down or take it off for use in this needy hour.
Letting down your hair is just a symbol of the hard work
required of you—
so let it down or take it out; you can put it back and
fix it up when this difficult task is through.
Really, Sister, hair is not the issue—you can have
real long hair or the tiniest 'fro.
Letting down hair or borrowing some is just the metaphor
for the extreme distance you always go!
Whether bald, shaved, dreaded, braided, permed,
wig-wearing, or honestly long and straight,
your inner strength and beauty are remembered when
the world testifies about how you handled what life
put on your plate!
You go, Girl!

Poem dedicated to my beauty technician, Pam Tardy

Extravagant Love!

ⵉⵀⵉⵀⵉ

.

T HE MOTHER EAGLE called to her babies, "Come from the nest. It's time to fly!" They were afraid.

The mother eagle called to her babies, "Come from the nest. It's time to fly!" They were terrified.

The mother eagle called to her babies, "Come to the edge. Just look and see." Trusting her, they came.

She pushed them over the edge.

And they flew!

Lent is about hearing the call to leave the nest of our comfort zones. Lent is about leaving the edge, where we look and see the possibilities, passing up the opportunities, refusing to take risks. Lent is about hearing the persistent call to come from the nest of comfort, doing more and becoming more than we have ever imagined. For Lent is our journey forward to meet God. Lent, like all of life, is a process of progress or movement; a seeking to advance closer to the One who loves us best.

Beloved, authentic life is moving past the traditional, the tried-and-true methods, and the status quo. Jesus uses Lent to call us to abundant life and to live a life of faith. Living a life of faith means not knowing the end of the story, but moving ahead into the unknown future, trusting the God of the journey.

One day I was reflecting on my life. I was trying to figure out the situations and to make sense of the nonsense I was dealing with. I'd get one piece of my life together and another piece would crumble. I'd stitch up, patch up, fix up one problem, and before I could relax and take it easy, another situation would wound my spirit, tear my confidence, and try to work my achy-breaky heart! So during my conversations with God, I was feeling pretty sorry for myself. While praying, I was voicing my complaints, fussing at God, really venting my anger about how my life was going. I distinctly remember some lines from my whining prayer: "God, nothing in my life is stable right now. Everything is tenuous and shaky. I feel like I'm walking on Jell-O."

And I clearly recall hearing in my spirit the affirmation: "Girlfriend, a life of faith is always shaky. You are walking on Jell-O!" Talk about a reality check. Talk about beginning to understand moving from the edge of life. Talk about starting to comprehend how God pushes us to make us fly. The baby birds would never have willingly jumped from the safety of the nest. Mother fed them. Mother brought them food. Mother was responsible for their safety. She took good care of them in the nest. But mother knew that they were destined to fly. Eagles are born to sail toward the bright heights of the sun. So she pushed them over the edge, and each of them declared, "I believe I can fly."

Six days before the Passover, Jesus wondered if any of his followers realized that his death was imminent. Six days before his death, the final exam for the group was fast approaching. And the Instructor was questioning whether or not the people in the class understood his lessons. They were yet looking for a Messiah. Six days before his crucifixion, they yet wanted a conquering king who would take over and kick tail. Six days before mob action was going to hang him high, the disciples wanted to overthrow the Roman government, set up a new political system, and be in charge. Six days before the religious-political system was going to stretch him wide, the disciples wanted a power broker and a miracle worker, whose signs and miracles would spellbind and mystify the world. Six days before he left them, he understood what the disciples wanted. But Jesus knew that the world had seen all of this before, and it had not changed the conditions. Sameness had not changed their foreparents. And it had not changed the lives of God's people. Jesus knew that his followers' reasoning and expectations were sheer insanity. You know the meaning of insanity! It's doing the same thing again and again, expecting different results. Jesus recognized that the disciples were comfortable in the nest. But he continued to call them to come to the edge and get a new perspective: "Come to the edge. Let life push you. I guarantee that you will learn how to fly."

Many of us watched both the wedding and the funeral of Princess Diana. There is always much pomp and circumstance when royalty gather for any purpose. These are always dignified affairs with a gathering of the social in-crowd. Any Jewish king would be crowned with great fanfare at the Temple in Jerusalem. There would be visiting potentates and regal dignitaries from every region of the known world. There would be much posturing and pecking order displays. There would be a huge crowd of male spectators in the inner court of the Temple. Non-Jews and women would be consigned to the outer courts. Only Jewish men would be able to watch as the reigning high priest anointed the new king as the one chosen by God to rule.

So Jesus, who always challenged the norms—this Jesus who had a history of doing the new and the different; this Jesus who always promoted and included the least, the last, and the lost—was ready to push his followers over the edge. Six days before he left them, and five miles outside Jerusalem, away from the madding crowd, Jesus gathered with his friends at the home of Simon the leper.

Like the HIV victims of our day, lepers were social outcasts. A leper was equivalent of the individual who has full-blown AIDS. Like AIDS, leprosy was contagious, and there was no cure. Lepers were not allowed in the Temple in Jerusalem. Lepers had to warn everybody that they were ritually unclean, not worthy to be in the company of others. So Jesus went where Simon was welcome, in his own home. Jesus goes to the place where outcasts are included. For even lepers and AIDS victims are precious to Jesus. Jesus loves with an extravagant love.

Brother Lazarus was eating with Jesus. The one whom Jesus raised from the dead after four days. The one who was called forth, bound in stinking grave cloths, was released and returned, shocked, but alive again, to his family. Six days before Jesus died, Lazarus was there as a testimony to the fact that death does not have the final word. When decay had claimed Lazarus as a victim, when his family was distraught and had given up hope, Jesus called him and restored him to life. The good news is that those of us yet dead in trespasses and sins are beautiful to Jesus. Jesus knows that liberation from a living death is available. Jesus is aware that the chains of our bondage can be released. Jesus loves even the walking, talking, living dead with an extravagant love.

Six days before Jesus was to die, Sister Martha was there. As always, she was doing the physical work thing. While Lazarus sat at the table, Martha served. It made no difference what house Martha went into, she was not able to break out of her box. Society placed limits on women, and she was comfortable in her limitations. Jesus loved Martha. She represents all of us who are stuck in life. She represents those of us who have a great case of the "I just can't help myself" syndrome. For even those of us who are stuck in our little ruts are of great worth to Jesus. He knows that there is more in us and there is more for us than the fences of limitations that we build around ourselves. Jesus loves with an extravagant love those of us who are afraid to color outside the lines.

Six days before he was to be tortured for your sin and mine, we find the outcasts, those called unfit, at the table with Jesus. The grateful dead were at the table. For Lazarus knew death would claim him again, but that day he was given a new lease on life. The ministering, serving, comfortable one was present. Martha would never be bold enough to sit at the table. She was satisfied with serving the table and eating from the scraps in the kitchen.

The good news is that Jesus sat with you and me that night. He knew we would be labeled minority, disadvantaged, inferior, and underprivileged. He looked down the corridor of time and saw that alcohol, drugs, sex, gambling, and food would bind us up and make us like Lazarus, the walking, talking, living dead. For when you're bound up and stinking, you are not living the abundant life. When you are stuck in the grave of "we've never done it this way before," Girlfriend, you're breathing, but you sure ain't living!

Jesus saw the evolution of women and affirmed our equal place at the table of life. Jesus wanted us to see a new day where servants would be in charge and would be able to sit down enjoying the fruit of their labors. For the good news is as the Bible declares it, and I believe it, "The last shall be first, and the first shall be last!" (Matt. 20:16). Women of color have been last on everybody's list since the world began. But it's our time now! Everybody else has come out of the box. And now it's our turn! Regardless of where we are in life, today Jesus loves us with an extravagant love.

So six days before the crucifixion, here's the picture: we are outside the Jewish anticipated city of Jerusalem, with a motley crew of misfits and society's rejects. The King of Glory sits and waits to see which disciple will fly. It's six days before Passover, he's five miles from meeting death, and this mother eagle says, "Come to the edge. Look and see."

See a woman named Mary enter a room filled with male disciples. See a woman named Mary carrying an expensive alabaster jar. See her crack this extravagant piece of art, filling the room with a sweet aroma. See a woman named Mary coming to the edge. Now Jesus is at a critical moment in his life. He knows death is certain. But do any of these, his closest circle, understand that? Does anyone honestly care about him and his needs?

Friends of mine, we all have critical moments in our lives. We all need to know there is somebody who loves us and can validate our lives. We all need somebody who will comfort us and love us without reservation and with extravagance. Ever had bad news come your way? You needed someone. Ever had to wait on a lab test to come back? You needed someone. Ever sat watching, waiting, wondering if the car would enter the driveway or whether the phone would ring? You needed someone. Ever been filled with the pain of grief or the despair of depression? You needed someone. Ever had to wonder whether your spouse was cheating with your best friend? You needed someone. Ever had to wonder if you were ever going to get a spouse or a best friend? You needed someone. Ever had to wonder how your child was going to end up in life? Ever had to wonder if you would or even could have a child in this life? Girlfriend, surely, you needed someone. And there is One who cares! Jesus is his name.

Six days before his death, Jesus needs someone, and along comes a woman named Mary. She comes and breaks open the alabaster jar filled with the embalming fragrance she'd more than likely purchased for her own death. The worth was equal to several years' wages. The jar alone was an object of art. Yet she breaks open the jar and walks over to pour this sweet perfume on Jesus. She *anoints* him as Messiah. She becomes his ministering angel. *She does the work of the high priest.* She is the only disciple who is ready to fly. His approaching death pushes her out of her nest of comfortable limits.

The people in the gathering sit dumbfounded and ignorant. They don't have a clue! She falls to her knees and begins to wipe his feet with her hair.

Rapunzel, Rapunzel, Sister, let down your hair. There is this hurting man in need of your tender care. Girlfriend, it's all right if your hair is paid for or even borrowed. Just let it down or take it out in this very needy hour. Letting down your hair is just a symbol of the difficult task required of you. So let it down or take it out. It can be fixed when this assignment is through. Really, Sister, hair is not the issue. You can have real long hair or even the tiniest 'fro. Letting down your hair is a metaphor for the distance women often have to go. So whether bald, shaved, dreaded, braided, permed, wig-wearing, or honestly long and straight, your inner strength and beauty are remembered when the world testifies about how you handle what life puts on your plate.

Sister Mary is not ashamed to let her hair down. Her body language says, "Oh, come let us adore him. He is Christ, the Lord!" Girlfriend takes a giant step forward toward difference. She leaps outside the limits. She jumps directly into risk taking, and that's when church really begins! Deacon Judas, the treasurer, begins to whine, trying to sound pious and religious. Brother Judas begins to criticize this unorthodox ministry of extravagant love. Judas begins to try and put her in her place. But Jesus says, "Leave her alone!"

Listen to Mark 14:6–9: "Leave her alone," said Jesus. "Why are you bothering her? She has done a beautiful thing to me . . . you can help the poor anytime. But you will not always have me. She did what she could. She poured perfume on my body beforehand to prepare for my burial. I tell you the truth, wherever the gospel is preached throughout the world, what she has done will also be told, in memory of her!"

Her extravagant love for Jesus became the deed that must be talked about every time we preach about the death and resurrection of our Christ. Her extravagant love became a deed of ministry that said to Jesus, in his critical moment, somebody got the lesson right. Her act of extravagant love translated her feelings of love into a ministry of love. She was the only person present who saw that Jesus had a critical need. He didn't need pats on the back for what he had accomplished in the past three years. He didn't need to be challenged about why he hadn't done things differently. He didn't need a bowl of warm soup and a fried chicken leg. What he needed was obvious, generous, active, and extravagant love poured out just for him. This woman, Mary, saw his need and she met it.

Jesus had come to earth and was born in a stable. His first knowledge of this bitter earth was the stinky manure of animals and the musty scent of humans who couldn't bathe regularly.

He lived for thirty-three and one-half years with stinky folks, in "da hood," who were always trying to throw stinking accusations at him as well as stab him in the back. Now he was preparing to die on Calvary's cross. And Golgotha's hill was high on a grave dump. So he died smelling the compacted garbage of the earth as well as the stench of our collective sin! All around him was the odor of filth and decay. From his birth to his death, garbage was his company. But Mary poured the sweet embalming fragrance on him, and it reminded him of heaven and home. With this gift of extravagant love, a sweet-smelling sacrifice, the precious Lamb of God was instantly carried, in his mind, to the pristine confines of heaven, where the walls are jasper and the streets are made of gold. The perfume Mary poured on Jesus reminded him that he was on his way home; mission accomplished!

As he became our broken body and our blood poured out for sin, Mary helped set the table. She did it because of her extravagant love. You and I have the same opportunity to show Jesus' extravagant love by activating our ministries where we live, work, socialize, and play. Ministry is our lifestyle, sisters. Ministry is not just the volunteer stuff we do in the name of the church. We can help the needy in the area. We can love one emotionally deprived child. We can clothe and feed the hungry of our area. We can visit the prisons and help those who are bound by drugs and alcohol. We must become mentors. We ought to be exemplary role models. Whatever's the best we have to offer, like Mary, we need to be serious about giving him the best we got!

We have to get up out of the nest. We have to move from the edge, where we sit and talk about what we're "gonna do," and what "oughta" be done! Lent comes to push us over the edge. The call of the cross is for us to take off and to fly! I believe I can fly, and "if I can help somebody with a word or song as I travel on, if I can show somebody where they're going wrong, then my living will not be in vain!"

I am persuaded that Sister Mary had to use self-talk to move past the limits of her fear. Mary had to talk herself into doing the different and the difficult. Girlfriend had to convince herself that this was an all right, okay, and necessary deed that she had to accomplish. Mary had to psych herself up, and I'm sure Woman Wisdom spoke to her in these words:

Go ahead, be determined to give him the best that you've got!
Love him with an extravagant love.
What you've got, pour on him.
Your determination will bless your life!

CAN WE TALK?

Letting down your hair is a symbol of freeing yourself to do the difficult and different. Your name may not be Mary and your hair may not be long, but you stand in a long and strong tradition of women who have done the difficult and the different. It's time for you to choose to do a new thing! If you continue to do the same things you've always done, you will receive the same results. So why not take a risk? Why not go for it? Why not try a change? It doesn't have to be anything big, drastic, or earth-shattering. What do you have that you can pour out onto the world? Perhaps it's volunteer skills that you can invest in a new and different setting. Perhaps it's time that you can use to take a new course in something fun. It might be as simple as taking a mental health day off from work to do something liberating. The issue is that there are some critical needs all around you. You see them. What will you choose to offer as an act of love? God is still looking for disciples who can fly!

Are you stuck at the crossroads wondering how to offer your gifts when they have been rejected, dissed, and tossed aside so many times before? We each know the story of somebody, somewhere who did something to hurt us or make our offering seem trivial. Mary knew what "da boys" thought about women in her world. She was well aware of how men treasure money and what it can buy. But she was determined to offer the best she had, not to the world, not to the group, but to the One who loved her best. When you offer yourself and your gifts, remember in whose name and for whose sake you offer them. Your offering blesses Jesus Christ!

Subtle Abuse

Jack and Jill went up the hill
to get their pails of water.
When Jack fell down and broke his crown,
Jill began to rule! She lived happily ever after!

Now I Lay Me Down
to Sleep . . .

⊱⊰⊱⊰

SHE HAD WAITED A long time for marriage. She was middle-
aged, professional, sophisticated, refined, and well employed. She owned her own home and car. She dressed well,
traveled extensively, and had vast knowledge of both men and
the world. Yet she chose to marry a crazy man. She was asleep.

She had waited a long time for marriage. She recognized his
moodiness and controlling anger. She saw the bizarre way he
handled relationships. Open eyes and Wisdom cautioned her
spirit, put a check in her eagerness, and warned her that "all
was not well." Yet she chose to marry a crazy man! She was
asleep.

The marriage was not good. Regardless of how she tried, he
didn't get better. Her excuses about him didn't even wash within
herself. He became more withdrawn and reclusive. His temper
tantrums, outbursts of anger, and excessive attempts to control
all of her free time became overwhelming. Yet she chose to stay
in a bad situation with a crazy man! She willingly remained
asleep.

His family knew he was crazy. They appreciated her supply-
ing him with some semblance of normalcy. He worked. He hated
everybody he worked with. He worked. He became more and
more obsessed with getting those he felt were out to get him.

He worked. This became his life. He worked. They worked to downsize his position. They succeeded. He began a fast descent.

Her ideals were shattered. Her dreams were destroyed. Her hope for marriage and a family had diminished. Her health began to suffer. Depression gripped her and would not let her go! She finally made the decision to leave him. She told him and his family that their days together were numbered. She tried to help him get things in order. She set a date for him to vacate her home. She decided to visit a friend while he moved out. She thought it was an amicable separation. She tried to forget that she had married a crazy man! She was waking up!

He called and canceled all his credit cards, bank accounts, and insurance benefits. He wrote ugly, nasty, hate-filled notes and hid them in various places around the house. He went into the bathroom and found several bottles of pills she had left behind. He took enough to do the job. Then he pulled the batteries out of a clock, indicating the time her plane departed, and set it on the nightstand in their bedroom. He took off all his clothes, lay face down on the floor, and died.

I pray the Lord my soul to keep . . .

It was several days before his decomposing body was discovered. She was called and returned home to a house in shambles. His family members were filled with escalating anger and grief. True to form, their anger was directed toward her: "How could you leave him?" "Didn't you recognize how ill he was?" "What kind of Christian are you?" Their attacks were vicious. Their charges were cruel and unkind. They decided she was not "worthy" to plan his memorial service. Yet she was the surviving spouse.

In the midst of her confusion, grief, and pain, she reached out to her pastors for assistance. They came. They were not trained to help. Suicide is a different and difficult animal to grasp. Its tentacles are far-reaching. Grief is not clear and pure. Questions are floating everywhere. Which one needs attention first? The pastors helped her design a regular worship.

She couldn't think. She couldn't articulate her pain. She didn't know which direction to take. She was lost in a maze, turning in circles, and seeking to understand, "Why?" Suicide brings its share of both assumed and implied guilt. There was overwhelming shame as others watched her with suspicion and fear. "Will you also go away in the same fashion?" seemed to be the unasked question! For many nights she wondered the very same thing! Every time she turned around, another note surfaced, pointing a finger of blame from beyond.

The day of the memorial arrived. There had been no family gathering beforehand. Church members were reluctant to visit since she'd remained in the home where he'd killed himself. The stench remained—physically, mentally, and emotionally. It affected her spiritually. She could not pray!

She recalls that during the period immediately after the suicide, the only prayers she heard were those offered when someone asked, "Can I pray with you?" She listened. She could not participate. She was living in a crazy situation. The only words that kept running through her head were, "Jesus loves me, this I know!" She couldn't recite it all. These six words were enough to see her through. It was her prayer. It carried her.

The memorial service was a fiasco! His family had an agenda and wanted to "speak their piece," in that place, despite her desire for an established and printed order of service. They were so irate that the pastors escorted her into a walk-in freezer as they tried to reason with the family's misdirected anger. She was a grieving widow, hidden in a locked room, while a gathered congregation waited in the sanctuary. "Jesus loves me, this I know!"

She didn't fall apart, lose it, or begin to yell and scream until weeks later. She held it in. She stuffed it. She denied her rage toward him. She kept people at bay, not wanting to deal with their questions. Her pastors came and called with prayers that did not console her. Finally, she returned to work, thinking life would return to normal. But she couldn't return to church.

Many days she dressed and drove to the church, sitting in her car, wanting to enter. But her former friends had distanced themselves, acting as if suicide was contagious! She even tried to enter the worship late. As she approached the door, put her hand on the knob, heard the music coming from within, she couldn't pull the doors open.

Her denomination required only two years of administrative training for pastors. Her pastors were a loving couple, decent and caring, but their pastoral care skills were lacking. Their ability to simply sit and cry with her was absent. They wanted to provide quick and easy answers. There were none. Yet "Jesus loves me, this I know," kept ringing through her head. It was her prayer. It was enough.

If I should die before I wake . . .

Only two people, a dear girlfriend and her goddaughter, made up her shrinking world. With them she could rant and rave. With them she could cry, wail, and question. With them she could "almost" be her authentic self. "Almost," for she felt like dying. "Almost," because she considered suicide. "Almost," due to the guilt and shame that were her constant companions. "Almost," since many days she doubted her sanity and salvation. "Almost," as the hole in her soul widened and her world shrank.

She had remained in her house. At the most inopportune times she continued to discover the notes he had hidden, in the most unlikely places. Of course they set her back from whatever small steps forward she had taken.

She decided to thoroughly clean house. She utilized a Dumpster and huge garbage bags as she went through old stuff, discarding both junk and painful memories. She ran across a brochure in a pile of neglected mail. It was a glossy, slick brochure, done in white with brilliant red bold letters. She glanced at it. She tossed it in the garbage. Wisdom whispered, "Pick it up again." She did.

It was an open invitation to a gathering for hurting women. It was a call to participate in worship, small groups, and plenaries focused on the issues that women face in life. It was a summons to healing circles, facilitated by women who specialized in pastoral care. It was a promise that listening would be done with an attitude of care. It was a pledge that cures would not be guaranteed, but caring was. It was an appeal to join voices, share tears, participate in prayers that would reach the heart of God! It was a mandate of the Holy Spirit that she advance from the pit of isolated gloom and begin a period of reclaiming ownership of her own soul. "Jesus loves me, this I know" was her prayer. It carried her to Daytona Beach, Florida, and the Woman to Woman Advance seminar!

I pray the Lord my soul to take . . .

Women gathered from across the country. The opening plenary began with a call to sisterhood and community. "The daughters of the healing God have gathered!" Sisters came with full awareness that pain and healing were the sole agenda items. With loving care, memory boxes were opened through liturgy, song, dance, and proclamation of God's Word.

Small groups were formed at random, asking sisters to share, work, and eat together in order to foster trust. It was revealed that family histories, life experiences, and cultural traditions met and merged often. Conversations had a life of their own and carried women in many unexpected directions. Laughter, silence, tears, and recall filled the spaces, connecting the sisterhood.

The healing circles unpacked pain. The healing circles allowed painful incidents to be explored, released. Anger that had simmered for too long was let go. Masks, covering broken hearts, were shed. Fading dreams were resurrected and dying hopes were given new life. The women were gentle with each other, for they saw themselves in others' stories. And layers of useless, dead dreams were thrown out as trash. Souls were reclaimed.

She was able to recognize many of the fairy tales upon which she had tried to base her life. She realized that all the things her mother and grandmothers had told her were not "truth" for her life. She, and many others, had carried too much junk around, locked away in the trunk of her memory. She allowed the sisters in her healing circle to inspect a lot of her stuff.

In this sacred space she discovered unearthed treasures within herself. Too often good and quality stuff is pushed down, stuffed under, or swept into the neglected and forgotten crawl spaces of our lives. As these sisters gathered, everything was open to scrutiny, question, challenge, and affirmation.

While sharing, new information could be received as gifts by sisters who'd never said a word. Some things were taken home to be used as options never before considered. For life is not just black *or* white. There are choices other than fight or flee. Just sitting, listening, sharing, and receiving the gift of care

allowed movement in her life. She saw the symbolic Dumpster
and garbage bags in the middle of the floor. She determined
there was a lot of useless baggage that needed to be trashed.
She invested in the process of reclaiming her soul!

If I should die before I wake, I pray the Lord my soul to take . . .

She gave her soul to the One who loved her best. She took
ownership of her one authentic possession, herself. She made
a conscious decision to move from that old place into a new
future in tomorrow. The pain no longer immobilizes her. There
is a rainbow in her sky. She's moved. She lives in a new place
filled with blues (calm) and yellows (*Sonshine*)! She's better,
not bitter. For the sisters gathered and assured her, "Jesus loves
you, this I know!"

CAN WE TALK?

I hate to get to this point known as The End! It seems as if
there is so much more I need to say. So much more you need to
glean for the journey that is ahead. But this is the last story at
this time!

I pray that you understand just how much our God loves
YOU! Every story has been preserved for you to see yourself,
gain knowledge so that you don't repeat the same mistakes, and
be able to claim movement for the days ahead. God loves you
just like you are! And the good news is that God loves us too
much to leave us like we are . . . asleep!

So a woman named Wisdom has brought us together for such
a time as this. I give God praise for this woman, our sister, our
guide, our leader in actualizing self-determination. It's time to
awaken from the fantasy that you've created. As my grandson,
Giraurd, says, "You need to wake up and smell the stench!" And
then my other grandson, Bear, says, "You had better bust you a
couple of moves!" I pray that the sisters who have met us in this
book have provided you with some alternative methods that will
work for you if you work them!

It's been my gift and joy to share this time with you. I thank
you for another opportunity to sit and chat with you like this. I
can see you. I'm with you in spirit. I've got your back in prayer.

Loving God, I pray for this my sister (and for my bold brother!).
I pray that Wisdom will lead them into new beginnings. I pray
that the Holy Spirit will empower them for bold living. I pray
that Wisdom will illumine their minds and that the Holy Spirit
will put running in their feet. I pray that Wisdom will provide
new direction and that the Holy Spirit will make their paths
plain. I pray for a new and fresh anointing upon their lives. And
I pray for all that concerns them.

Gentle Savior, enfold them, embrace them, let them know
without a shadow of a doubt that "Jesus loves me, this I know."
And let that knowing not be remote, academic, and linear. Let
them experience your working on the inside to make alive, real
and authentic, difference on the outside. Let them experience
knowing you through your direct involvement in their lives. I
pray that they learn to be bodacious, wise women. I pray that
they TAKE courage! I pray that they will bust a couple of moves,
knowing that you have already moved on their behalf.

God, get the glory out of the time they have invested with you
in prayerful reading. Let the Living Word become the Bread of
Life within them. Take them from where they are today to the
heights you have preordained for them. In the name of the Powerful Christ I pray with thanksgiving and confidence. Until we
meet face-to-face with you! May it be so now and always.

Shalom, my friends, Shalom!
Sista Linda H. Hollies

Other Books from United Church Press and The Pilgrim Press

⊢⊣⊢⊣

TAKING BACK MY YESTERDAYS
Lessons in Forgiving and Moving Forward with Your Life
LINDA H. HOLLIES
0-8298-1208-3/Paper/176   pages/$10.95

"A must-read book! Linda Hollies has successfully combined personal honesty and solid biblical storytelling to teach us how to forgive and let go of yesterday. She gives us new tools for building a satisfying tomorrow. The prayers will inspire you. The principles will encourage you. The psalms will direct your path. Linda Hollies, what a blessing you are!"
—Iyanla Vanzant, author of *In The Meantime* and *Yesterday I Cried*

"With Hollies' reassuring guidance, readers will be able to return to the place of pain, confront those who were involved in causing the pain, and invite God's healing power to bring forth forgiveness."—*Spiritual Book News*

"This remarkable little book is one of the most precious gifts we can give ourselves or a loved one this year. . . . *Taking Back My Yesterdays* is a lifetime of wisdom bound in a pocket-sized book. It is a hospital full of healing small enough to carry constantly. It should be kept close at hand and freely dispensed among our friends as a token of love, as an offer of mercy."
—*Informed Resource*

JESUS AND THOSE BODACIOUS WOMEN
Life Lessons from One Sister to Another
LINDA H. HOLLIES
0-8298-1246-6/Paper/224   pages/$11.95

"Define bodacious as 'unmistakable, remarkable, and note-worthy' and you've a good working description of Hollies as well as the biblical women she discusses in this essay compilation. Earmarking each new chapter with a portion of scripture, Hollies tells the stories of an assortment of biblical women. With flavorful anecdotes, readers will get a new take on the woman at the well found in John 4 as Hollies admonishes 'sistergirls' to look to God for self-respect. . . . Hollies puts gusto, real heart and vivid imagination into every tale."
—*Publishers Weekly*

Humorous and intuitive, delightful and poignant, the work of Linda Hollies has struck a chord in the lives of many readers. In *Jesus and Those Bodacious Women*, Hollies serves up new spins on the stories of biblical women. From Eve to Mary Magdalene, portraits of the bodaciousness of the many matriarchs of the Christian tradition will prove to be blessings for readers young and old.

DAUGHTERS OF DIGNITY
African Women in the Bible and the Virtues of Black Womanhood
LAVERNE MCCAIN GILL
0-8298-1373-X/Paper/176   pages/$16.95

To help African American women erase the hurtful and inaccurate stereotypes that confront them and to reclaim a connection with their deep ethical roots and moral heritage, LaVerne Gill shares the stories of foremothers who were supported by justice, love, faith, wisdom, and perseverance—virtues that empowered them to have strong families and productive careers. Gill also offers historical and contemporary role models, including Sojourner Truth and Rosa Parks, and gives suggestions for self-evaluation and narratives on contemporary programs to reestablish an ethic of black womanhood in the community.

BLACK WOMEN IN THE IMAGE OF GOD
DOROTHY WINBUSH RILEY, ED.
0-8298-1257-1/Paper/128   pages/$21.95

Bestselling author Dorothy Winbush Riley has assembled a rich and varied collection of photography, fine art, and sculpture depicting the past, present, and future of women of African descent. In this remarkable book, vibrant full-color and black-and-white images portraying the tenderness and strength of people of the Diaspora are coupled with words from the Bible and quotes from such noted writers as Maya Angelou, Margaret Walker, James Weldon Johnson, and Toni Morrison.

A companion volume, *Black Men in the Image of God*, is also available.
0-8298-1256-3/Paper/128   pages/$21.95

To order these or any other books from The Pilgrim Press or United Church Press, please call or write to:

THE PILGRIM PRESS
700 Prospect Avenue East
Cleveland OH 44115-1100

Phone orders: 1-800-537-3394
Fax orders: 216-736-3713

Please include shipping charges of $3.50 for the first book and $0.50 for each additional book.

Or order from our Web sites at www.pilgrimpress.com or www.ucpress.com.

Prices are subject to change without notice.